# Mastering Amazon Ads:
# An Author's Guide

by
Brian D. Meeks

ISBN: 978-1-942810-15-5

For Howard and Sandy, their love and support made me an author. Their wonderful brains gave me the genes to figure all this stuff out.

# Contents

# Chapter One: Introduction

Getting started in anything new, like using Amazon Marketing Service (AMS) ads successfully, can be scary. Even writing instructions to help someone start something new comes with its fair share of trepidation.

"Don't worry. I've got this," he said, more to himself than anyone.

Later in this book I'm going to cover many aspects of marketing: how to improve your ad's performance, return on investment (ROI), some of the misconceptions about Amazon ads, and dozens of other pieces to the puzzle.

What I hope to do is to ease you into mastering Amazon ads in a way that won't be scary and will help you build your understanding of how to analyze results to allow for continued improvement.

Let's begin with what type of ad to run. Nearly everyone I talk to about Amazon ads believes that one should only run Sponsored Product ads, heretofore called "keyword" ads for simplicity. There seems to be a consensus that Product Placement ads don't work.

I have spent over $42,000 on Product Display (Interest) ads, and they've generated over $162,000 in sales and KU page read revenue. They work for me. I have a theory about how so many people arrived at such an erroneous conclusion, which we will discuss later in this book. The point is they do work.

There are two other reasons to use Product Display (Interest) ads:

1. They're super easy to set up.
2. They're the only ones that actually run on people's Kindles.

This book will teach you about all the different ways to run ads. Right now, though, as I'm sure you're anxious to get going, I'm going to give you a "starter" set of ads to run.

My goal for the readers is to get you familiar with the ads and to make decisions on bid levels and budgets that are super conservative. It is easier and less terrifying if you only dip your toes in the water to start.

We will have you run four ads to start, one of each type. If you've followed other people running ads, you may have seen that some people build keyword lists of 500, 1000, even 12,000 for a single book. Initially, we're going to set our sights much lower. In a later chapter, I'll go into detail about how to build a massive keyword list.

Some of the questions I hear most often follow, and I'm going to begin by giving my short answer without explanation to keep things simple. More details will follow later in the book on each subject.

# Chapter Two: Start Small and Test

## Start Small and Test

This seems like the sort of advice that doesn't need mentioning, but it's absolutely true.

When I began running Amazon ads in early 2015, it was only available to those who sold their books exclusively on Amazon (also called being "exclusive.") All my titles were "wide" (meaning I had published them on Amazon as well as on Nook [Barnes and Noble], iTunes/iBooks, Kobo, etc.), but I wanted to give it a test. I pulled one of my books, a thriller, out of being wide and made it "exclusive". This book was chosen mostly because it never sold, and I rarely ran any sort of promotion for it. My thriller, *A Touch To Die For*, was the perfect test subject.

At the time, the price point was $3.99. The first thing I did was look at the suggested bids, .37 – .48 per click. As of the writing of this book, the suggested bid is .15 – .25. Regardless, I knew that my margin was about $2.75. I also knew that if I bid .37 then I would need to have one sale every 7.4 clicks.

There wasn't anything about the sales history of this book that indicated my conversion rate would be anywhere close to that. The cover, which I keep thinking I'll change, is only fair, and as I later found out, the description copy was pretty weak. So, running ads for this book had a lot going against it.

Since there were rarely any sales, I decided I'd pick a crazy low bid and see what happened. I went with .03 on the ad and I forgot about it. About a month later there had been a few dollars in spend. It was barely noteworthy, but my sales were up by four over what I had most months. Now, to be fair, this wasn't anything close to statistically significant data. All of those sales could have been outliers. (Note: The reporting wasn't as good with regard to the sales as it is now.)

I decided to try another advertisement and this time I bid .04. The results were fine. I had spent more and had more impressions. It was the impressions I started to pay attention to because they told me how often the book was getting exposure. I encourage you to watch the impressions closely on your ads. This number tells you a bunch. We'll cover what one learns from impressions later.

The point was that this book that had been making less than $10 per month was now making $20 per month profit once the .04 ads started to get going. I decided to pull my next worst performing book from being wide. It was a YA.

This title's advertisement wasn't as good as the thriller's, but it made a little money. And then it didn't. And then it did. Over a month, it was profitable but only just barely. The thriller was doing much better.

When Amazon switched the Kindle Unlimited (KU) payout from a lump sum to page reads, my heart leapt. This was a big deal from not only a revenue point but also from a data analysis perspective.

Imagine you've got an advertisement, and let's say it shows to 5,000 people, though many of them probably don't notice it. But let's say that 50 people click on the ad. One click per 100 impressions (on the Product Display ads) is considered to be a better than average ad in my book.

Now, carrying that through, let's imagine that the bid is .04. So, we've spent $2.00. Let's say that our weak cover and rather average description converts at 1 in 25. That's two sales or $5.50 in revenue on a price point of $3.99.

Calculating ROI is easy. (Revenue – Ad spend)/Ad spend, so $5.50 – $2.00 = $3.50. We divide that by $2.00 to get a return on investment of 175%. That's a great return.

Put another way, the equation can read: (The pile of money made – the pile of money spent)/(the pile of money spent). And that's how you get your ROI.

Okay, that's all well and good, but let's look at a similar scenario. Let's say that there are 10,000 impressions and 100 clicks. For this attempt, we've spent $4.00 and after two weeks, our report says we've had zero sales. Well, that's a bummer, but is it?

There have been 100 people who have read the description and some of those people are subscribers to Kindle Unlimited. Let's say that four of those people decide to give your book a read.

Now, we get paid per page read. In the case of this book, the KENPC (Kindle Edition Normalized Page Cout) is say 300 and you check and sure enough you've had 1,200 page reads. So, that confirms our suspicion that your advertisement yielded some new readers even if they didn't buy the book.

To calculate the ROI in this instance, take the number of pages (1,200) times the rate per page. It varies from month to month. In the time I've been doing this I've seen it as low as .0042 and as high as .00537. Let's use .005. That means our book earned $6.00 or an ROI of 50%. That's not as good as 175%, but it's still pretty darn good.

These examples are simple versions of what I was seeing with my tests. When the income from page reads was calculated in, my thriller was doing better than I thought, and the YA was doing okay.

I made the decision to pull all of my books from wide and go exclusive.

There are several benefits to being exclusive. One gets to run either Free days or Countdown Deals during the 90-day commitment. I'll write a bit about those features at the end of the book in an appendix.

The other big benefit was that one could advertise their book. That benefit no longer exists because the advertising platform is now open to everyone. So, even if you're wide, you can still advertise on Amazon, which is really nice for Indie authors everywhere.

Did this change hurt my revenue from increased competition? Yes, it dampened my results, but I still make more money than I did at my day job by a long shot. You don't need to cry for me Argentina. I'm fine.

But, that is just one example of how things can change and one needs to adapt.

Anyway, back to how I started small and grew. Once I had all my books exclusive, I began running ads for the first book in the mystery series, because I figured I'd get people into the series on book one and let them move on to the other three books. At the time, I didn't have my science fiction series.

My previous best month of sales was one where I had a 99-cent BookBub promotion, and I earned $2,300 in net profit. My first full month of Amazon ads, bidding mostly .05 per click, I cleared $3,000 after deducting the costs of the ads. The next month I cleared $7,000.

My best month came in December 2015 with $15,300 in sales (and KU revenue) on $4,000 in spend.

Then January 5, 2016 came and something horrible happened. I'll tell that story later. But I survived and adapted.

The idea is that your book is unique in the cover design, the advertising copy (description), and how many reviews (social proof) you have, and all of those things impact the decision-making process of the people who click through your ads.

You will want to download my Excel workbook and start slow so you can learn what works and what doesn't.

## Types of Ads

There are two types of advertisements through Amazon Marketing Services (AMS):

1. Sponsored Products: These ads use keywords to determine when they will be shown and are displayed in search results and on product detail pages. Two options are possible for targeting: automatic targeting where Amazon picks the keywords and manual targeting where you enter your own keywords.

2. Product Display Ads: These ads display on the product detail pages and on Kindle e-readers. One may target by product or interest.

It's important to understand that these two types of ads behave differently and potentially reach different eyeballs. If an author only has a Sponsored Product advertisement because they have figured out a great list of keywords, then the people who regularly do searches on Amazon will see the ad. But what about the folks who mostly read on their Kindle and find their books from native ads on their device? I've gotten many emails from people after they've read one of my books, and I always ask how they found out about it. The number one response is they saw an advertisement on their Kindle.

You will want to experiment with both types of ads.

When one compares Sponsored Product ads to Product Display ads, another interesting thing jumps out: the number of impressions it requires to get one click.

They are vastly different.

Let me tell you a little bit about the advertisements I've run to show the size of the data pool from which I'm garnering my results.

I've submitted 677 ads and all but 5 were approved. Of the 672 remaining ads, 87 of them never had a single impression. That happens sometimes. I don't worry about it.

Of the 585 that are left, 169 of those ads never had a single click. Most of these ads had very few impressions, though one of the sponsored product (keyword) ads did have 2,389 impressions. That it didn't have one click tells me it was a poor ad. Most of the ads that never got a click (147) had fewer than 100 impressions.

That leaves us with 416 ads. Seven of those are still

pending review because I just ran them, so my data set consists of 409 ads.

The breakdown between the two types of ads follows: 37 are Sponsored Product ads and 370 are Product Display ads. My lifetime spend on the Sponsored Product (keyword) ads is $106.63, and the spend on the Product Display ads is $41,899.49 (as of May 2017).

One might wonder why there is such a discrepancy.

There are two reasons. One, the Sponsored Product ads have only been around since the middle of 2016. They are a new type of ad, and as such, I've run fewer of these ads. Secondly, the reason I focus on the Product Display ads is they have a much better click-through ratio, which was the point of this section. So, let's look at the numbers of the two types of ads.

IMPORTANT: Writing numbers can sometimes be confusing if one isn't used to dealing with decimals. In the following examples, I compare Fiction and Non-Fiction Books. I wrote the Fiction numbers using a % sign and then the Non-fiction numbers using just a decimal point so you can see the difference.

An example is that .24% = .0024. They are the same number. I've done it both ways because it can be easy to get confused if you're looking at data one way and are more familiar with the other. Read the following sections and spend the time to become competent with both ways of writing the numbers. (I know I'm being a pain, but do it anyway.)

Click-through rate = CTR

Fiction

Short Answer:

1. Sponsored Product CTR = 769 impressions for a click
2. Product Display CTR = 142 impressions for a click

Sponsored Product CTR range = .04% – .24%, with 68% of the ads falling between .08% – .16% CTR. The mean is .13. In other words, on average it takes around 769 impressions for a single click.

Product Display CTR = .11% – 2.8%, with 68% of the ads falling between .56% – .84%, with a mean of .7%. So it takes 142 impressions to yield a click.

Non-Fiction

Short Answer:

1. Sponsored Product CTR = 978 impressions for a click
2. Product Display CTR = 196

For this data I used my co-author on a number of non-fiction books, Honorée Corder's Amazon ad data. I used the same methodology as for my own ads. She had 64 Sponsored Product ads and 87 Product Display ads.

Sponsored Product CTR Range = .00011 (3 clicks in 26,102 impressions) – .0042 with 68% of the ads falling between .00059 (42 clicks in 231,787 impressions) – .00158. The mean is .00102 or one click in every 978.

Product Display CTR Range = .00029 (3 clicks on 10,270 impressions) – .025. Again, looking at one standard deviation from the mean, 68% were in the range between .00165 and .00727. The mean CTR was .00508 or one click in every 196 impressions.

Comparing the two, it seems that for these two groups of data, the CTR is slightly better overall on fiction than non-fiction. It should be noted that the ad copy across both sets of ads is similar because Honorée and I work on them together. Any deficiencies I have with regard to my ad-writing abilities should show up across both sets. Conversely, if I'm doing something right, it's probably reflected in both ad groups, too.

This is important because you'll want to judge the efficiency of your ad copy based upon the CTR for each type separately. If you have an expectation that all your ads will have a CTR of .7 but you're mostly running Sponsored Product (keyword) ads, then you'll think the ads are doing poorly when they may be doing well for that ad type.

One more thing regarding the differences between these two ads and why I've spent so little on Sponsored Product ads, when Amazon rolled this new ad type out, there just weren't that many impressions to be had. I suspect, as all companies do, when it was new they didn't roll it out fully. It can take just as much time and energy on a Sponsored Product ad and sometimes more if you really spend a lot of time figuring out keywords. For me, at the time, it wasn't worth the effort.

I'm now convinced these ads I avoided are now an excellent method of growing sales.

I've begun to run a whole new batch of each type of ads just for the purposes of research for this book. I do know though that even though there appears to be more impressions available, the CTR is still much worse for Sponsored Product than Product Display.

Fiction vs. Non-fiction

Both fiction and non-fiction titles can generate sales from ads. There is, however, a difference in the total revenue from Kindle Unlimited between fiction and non-fiction and it's substantial.

The short answer is that KU subscribers are mostly fiction readers. A nice bump in sales from a fiction ad will then see a corresponding jump in the number of page reads the following day. Page reads always lag behind because not everyone buys a book and reads it in its entirety in the same calendar day. This is also why you'll notice it takes longer for page read numbers to decline after a sudden drop in sales because your ad spend has tanked. Yes, ad spend declining is part of the game. We'll get into that more later.

A similar bump in sales for non-fiction will see a much smaller bump in page reads.
Also, with fiction more than non-fiction, boxed sets are popular. Because of the number of pages in a three- or four-book boxed set, a nice jump in sales for the set will yield an even longer and more prolonged increase in page reads.

Boxed sets are great when the ads are working for them.

So, we know there are two types of ads. Now, it's time to look at how one runs an advertisement for their book.

# Chapter Three: Your First Ads

## Running Your First Advert

Assuming you have multiple books and are unsure which one to choose, let me make a suggestion or three.

1. If all of your titles are single books, then choose the one with the highest price point.

2. If you have one book at $2.99 and one at $4.99, choose the latter as you have greater margin.

3. If you have a boxed set, choose it over a single book because presumably it has a price point of $8.99 to $9.99, so you have a lot more margin and if you're exclusive to Amazon, the page reads will be fantastic.

These are suggestions for those just starting out. This

method is for your first ads. After you get the hang of it and can write effective copy, you may find it is better to run ads on a $2.99 first book in a series because you know the read through is 80% to the second book, and of those people, 95% read all the books in the series. If there are four books in the series then you'll make much more profit focusing on the first book, even if the ad seems to be losing a little bit of money.

I'll explain how to estimate read through later to help you make those decisions.

Okay, you've decided on your book. Let's say the title is *Battleship Bacon*, a story of space pirates who enjoy a good BLT from time to time. I would love it if that truly was the title of your book. Since I haven't written a book by that title, I'll be using *A Touch To Die For.*

We will run one advertisement for each of the two types of ads with each one using two methods for a total of four ads.

Ad One

1. Log onto Kindle Direct Publishing. This is where you go when you want to check on your sales.

2. Click on Reports.

3. Click on Ad Campaigns. This will open up a new tab. The first page is Advertising Campaigns, which at this point, if you're making your first ad, you won't have any approved ads, so this page will be blank. There is an orange "New Campaign" button. Find it.

4. Click the New Campaign button.

5. Choose a campaign type. Your two choices are Sponsored Products and Product Display ads. We will be starting with Sponsored Products. Click it!

6. Once you've clicked, a box will come up that allows you to pick your book. If you don't see any of your books, which is likely at the beginning, you'll need to use the search feature to find your book. You may search by ASIN, product name (book title), or keywords. Find the book *Battleship Bacon*. (Okay, that book doesn't exist. Yet. You'll be finding one of YOUR books.)

7. Hit the "Select" button next to your book.

8. Here we will be setting the campaign name, budget, and duration. It's important to NOT leave the default Campaign Name in there because later, when you're using the Excel workbook, you'll need to fill out a table with your

campaigns. It will be MUCH easier if the naming convention is something that makes it obvious which book is being advertised.

Example: ATTDF Spon Jan 2017 (1), this is how I do it. So it reads *A Touch To Die For*, Sponsored, Month and Year, and then in parenthesis the number of the ad. If it's my first one, I use (1), etc.

If you screw up and use the default, it won't be the end of the world, it will just mean that when you're looking at your ads you'll need to refer to the Excel table to be able to tell what they are and that's a pain. It is better to have it be clear.

Okay, so you've given your ad a name.

Great, now we need to talk about budgets.

For the first one, we're going to start small, but later in another chapter we'll talk about this some more. I would start with $5.00 or a little higher.

You'll then be asked if you prefer to "Run campaign continuously starting today or select a date range". I prefer continuously, but that's just me.

Ad One Continued:

1. Select Targeting. For the first ad, we'll choose "Automatic Targeting." You'll be doing "Manual Targeting" in the next ad.

2. Cost-Per-Click bid. This is the most important decision you'll need to make. If you bid too high, you'll have a tough time getting a profitable ad, but if you bid too low, your ad may not get that many impressions. Also, the correct bid that's profitable today may not be profitable next month. Or, it may be that next month you can bid less and get the same number of impressions. This business is seasonal and you'll be much more profitable if you're constantly testing.

3. Let's bid .15. (Note: DO NOT PUT 15 because THAT'S $15.00 per click. Make sure you put POINT ONE FIVE) Sorry, I didn't mean to yell, but it's really easy to make an expensive blunder.

4. Write your ad copy. This is the second hardest part of the ads business. The copy you write definitely impacts how many people click. I'm not an expert copywriter, but I have been studying it through sites like Copyblogger and books like Sugarman's, *The Adweek Copywriting Handbook:The Ultimate Guide to Writing Powerful Advertising and Marketing Copy from One of America's Top Copywriters*. I've picked up a

few things that have really improved my ads.

Link to buy Sugarman book
Http://briandmeeks.com/ams-mastering-amazon-ads-links/

I try to work one or two of these four words into each ad: You, Because, Now, Instantly. I read an article saying they were powerful and then tested it. The results were clear that they did improve the CTR.

It should be noted that what comes after the "because" isn't as important as what comes before. It's something about that word that makes people click, as if the word "because" means there is a justification. I'm just speculating but it does seem to work.

So, write your ad copy. Try to start with a short punchy sentence. For *A Touch To Die For,* I might use "A serial killer is born. And it's all for show. You'll be hooked by this thriller because everyone loves a page turner."

Here's one I used for *Henry Wood Detective Agency,* the first book in my detective series:

"Do you love a mystery? Do you like clever dames? You'll love this smart noir detective novel with a twist, because it has shades of Bogart and Bacall."

Let's look at the copy. The first question is only five words and they are so short that a person just glancing at the copy will read it even if they don't want to.

The idea is the first statement or question should be a hook that gets them to want to read what comes next.

"Do you like clever dames?"

This bit speaks to the era for the book. It takes place in 1955. Old dime store detective novels always used words like "dames". It isn't a word that would be used in a modern novel, so that tells the shopper a little more about the book.

Then we use the word "you" in a way that is speaking to the reader and we're telling them that they will love this smart noir detective (again, noir detective, speaks to the time period) novel with a twist because it has shades of Bogart and Bacall." There's that word "because".

If you don't know who Humphrey Bogart and Lauren Bacall are, that's okay. You're not the target market. If you enjoyed movies like The Maltese Falcon and Casablanca, you'll know Humphrey Bogart. If you liked To Have and Have Not, well that was the movie where one of the greatest Hollywood romances in history began. Heck, if you enjoy the song Key Largo by Bertie Higgins, you'll know the line "Honey I was your hero and you were my leading lady...We had it all...Just like Bogie and Bacall...Staring in our own late, late show, sailing away to Key Largo."

If none of that sounds familiar, that's okay...I'm old. The point is, this ad is designed to evoke memories and trigger actions in people who DO know the references, because they will like my book.

Writing good ad copy takes practice. The more you think about copy writing, the better you'll get at the skill. It's worth the time and effort.

Also, if a person is truly intrigued by your copy, then they will likely give your description a better read, and thus, have a greater chance of deciding to buy (or download through KU if you're in Select).

The last step is to look at the preview at the bottom. It's always a good idea to read your ad copy out loud. It helps to find mistakes. An ad will get rejected if there is a single error.

Final Step: Do you like your first ad? Okay, hit "Submit Campaign for Review" or if you're not quite ready, you may "Save as draft."

Typically, the people who review the ads will get them approved (or rejected) within 24 - 48 hours. It's a bit slower in November and December because of the holidays. I know I run more ads between Thanksgiving and the end of the year.

The official line is 72 hours, but they seem to always do better than that. Good job Amazon ad reviewers.

If your ad does get rejected, all is not lost. The ad will appear at the top of all the approved ads in a separate little section. The status will be "REJECTED." You'll have received an email that generally explains the reason for the rejection. I had one, once, where I spelled "the" using the rare ancient Latvian spelling "teh". All I had to do was edit the ad and fix the mistake.

It should be noted that while your advertisement is in "Pending review" status, you'll not be able to get into edit it. If you catch a mistake, you'll just have to wait until the soul crushing rejection lands in your inbox proclaiming to the world that you're a failure and a disappointment to your parents, siblings, and the Pope.

Actually, it's not that bad.

Ad Two

The first five steps are the same. This is like a pop-quiz. Can you make it through step five?

Good job. Now, it's time to pick the book. Okay, now you've selected your book. I'll be using the same one from the first ad.

Let's continue:

1. Campaign Name. Remember, you want to name it something that is easy to read and understand in the future. I'm doing another ad on my thriller, *A Touch To Die For*, so the name of the ad is ATTDF Jan 2017 (2).

2. Choose your budget. In Chapter 7, I discuss budgets and scaling more deeply but for now just go with the same amount you did on the last one.

3. Duration, choose "Run campaign continuously starting today"

4. Select a targeting Type. This time we're going to select manual.

5. Choose a CPC (cost per click). The default is .25, but I'll be going with .12 because the price point on my thriller is $4.99.

6. Suggested Keywords. Some of the suggested keywords for my book are suspense thriller, crime thriller, crime thriller novels, crime suspense. At

this point it is probably worth reading through the suggested keywords and deciding which ones you want to use. I hit the orange "Add all" button, which then selected all 19 key words.

Now, you may want to add some more keywords. If you look below the "Add keywords and bids for your search campaign" you'll see two tabs. You're on the tab called "Add suggested keywords," next to it is the tab "Add your own keywords."

Here you'll be able to type in a keyword and choose a bid for it. The bid doesn't need to be the same as the others. If you wanted to choose "United States" as a keyword and bid .25 for that one, while all the others are at .12, that's just fine.

I'm adding they keywords murder, serial killer, and conspiracy manually and bidding .12 for each. To do that I simply type in each keyword(s) on its own separate line and change my bid. Then I hit "Add."

You may put in lots of keywords. I have an author friend who has a list of over 600 he uses. I've heard tales of a woman with 12,000. You are limited to 1,000 in a single ad. It takes time. For now, let's keep working on this ad. You have three last steps:

1. Write your ad copy. Now, I would suggest for

these first four ads you use the same ad copy, so you can compare their performance.

2. Scroll up and double check your work. I sometimes, when I'm in a hurry, forget step 1, Campaign Name, and so I always double check this part.

3. If it's good, then hit the "Submit campaign for review" orange button.

Well done.

## Ad Three

1. Choose a campaign type. Choose Product Display Ads this time.

2. Select a book to advertise. You'll choose the same book as the previous two ads.

3. Target your ad. The two choices are "By product" and "By interest." We're going to choose "By product" for this one.

4. Select products to target. You may search by keyword, product name, UPC, or ASIN. I tend to go with the author names and hit "search." I'll start with Lee Child. This is the point where you

want to think about the types of books your readers like, though technically, it doesn't have to be books.

If the book you're advertising is *Best Back Yard BBQ Secrets* you might choose to do a search on "grill" and could then add "Weber 10020 Smokey Joe 14-Inch Portable Grill by Weber"

This is an area where creativity pays off.

I'm going to pick a few more authors and then move on. The next one I searched on was James Rollins. I used the "Add all on this page" method to move them over to my list. It stands at 60 now after these two authors.

One should note that just because you do a search on Charlotte Bronte, it may return books that were NOT written by her. It's always a good idea to scroll through the list and make sure they're the products where you want your book's ad to show up.

At this point, I should mention that though we are running ads to improve our Kindle sales, I do select print versions, too. And it will, occasionally, lead to a print sale for me.

If you're having trouble thinking of products (books and authors, possibly grills), then simply go to Amazon and start with your first author. Let's say your books would be enjoyed by Michael Crichton fans. Do a search and find one of his books. Then, below the description you'll see "Customer Who Bought This Item Also Bought," which we call "Also Boughts" for short. I see Lincoln Child, Robin Cook, Dan Browns, Ken Follett, and Douglas Preston, all just on the first page. There are twenty pages for the book *Dragon Teeth: A Novel.*

That's where I find my authors. I've quickly added a total of 251 keywords.

The next three steps are going to start to look familiar. That's a good thing.

1. Choose your campaign settings, Campaign Name. I'll use ATTDF Jan 2017 (3) Product. You'll notice that I added "Product" to my name.

2. Cost-per-click bid (CPC). This time I'm going for 0.08 (eight cents), to see if that gets any impressions. The "Average bid is $0.29 - $0.36" according to Amazon.

3. Campaign Budget. This is different from the Sponsored (Keyword) ads you've already run. You are not choosing a "Daily Budget." Instead, you're saying how much you want to spend over the entire campaign.

I'm choosing $1200.00, but I don't expect to spend much of that at the 8-cent bid.

If I were to guess, I'll probably spend between $1.00 and $300.00 over the life of the ad. Again, I go into much greater detail on budgets in Chapter 7.

Okay, three more steps:

1. Date Range. The default is two months from today. You'll notice it pre-fills those dates. They are fine and I just leave them as is before moving on to Pacing.

2. You may choose between "Run campaign as quickly as possible" and "Spread campaign evenly over its duration. "I always pick " as quickly as possible."

3. Customize your ad. This is different than the previous ads, too.

You have both a Headline, where you're limited to 50 characters, and a Text, which gives you 150 characters.

I tend to use the headline as my first line in the text. As an example:

Headline:

The evolution of a serial killer is a slow thing.

Text:

The evolution of a serial killer is a slow thing. This thriller will keep you turning pages well past your bedtime.

It is the second bit, the "Text" that you really want to nail.

Last Step: Preview your ad. You may click on the various sizes to see what the ad looks like. The ad sizes are 270x200, 300x250, and 980x55. With each one, you may click on the "Where will my ad appear?" And to see the ad as it would look on the Amazon site. It's not necessary that you do this, but having a good idea of how the ads are displayed is worthwhile.

If you're ready and you've reviewed your ad to make sure everything is the way you intend, then go ahead and submit.

Ad Four

Okay, this is the ad that I have the most experience with. Of the four, it's been my bread and butter for over two years.

1. Choose Product Display Ads.

2. Select the book you wish to advertise.

3. Choose "By Interest"

4. Select "Interest" to target

The reason, I believe that this type of ad is so successful is because it's the only one of the four that is displayed on Kindle e-readers. Sometimes when the ad pops up, it covers the entire screen (when it's the Kindle Screensaver). Your book isn't competing with any other ads. It has been delivered by Amazon based upon the interests you'll pick in Step 4.

I'm creating an ad for my thriller, so I click on the down arrow by "Mystery, Thriller & Suspense." Next I click on Conspiracies, Kidnapping, Murder, and Vigilante Justice, which are the interests that make the most sense for this book.

Each time you select an interest it is moved over to the Reader Interest Added box. If you decide you want to remove an interest you've selected, simply click on it and it will move back to All Reader Interests.

Keep at it; you're doing great.

1. Campaign Name. I'm going with ATTDF Jan 2017 (4) Interest as my name.

2. Enter your Cost-per-click bid. This time I'm going with eight cents

3. Campaign Budget. You'll want to go with a similar budget to what the other ads you've run have, but I'm going with $1200.00 (Note: It's not as scary as it looks because at such a low bid, there will likely not be that much action. If you bid .25 cents, you may spend a lot quickly and it may NOT be profitable. Basically, I'm going for the leftover impressions on this one. That being said, if Amazon wanted to spend $1200.00 of my money, I'd be thrilled.)

4. Date Range. It's set at two months and I'm fine with that so I don't change a thing.

5. Pacing. The default is "Run campaign as quickly as possible" which is also what I wanted.

6. Customize Your Ad

Headline: I usually write this first and then use it in the text portion. "The evolution of a serial killer takes time."

Text: This is the bit that shows up on the Kindles. "The evolution of a serial killer takes time. He's leaving the choosing of victims up to an unsuspecting author who has no idea he's involved." Note: I have nine characters remaining.

Despite having some leftover characters, you'll notice that not everything shows up on the Kindle Screensaver version. I assume that's because people have their Kindles set up differently and there are different models. I've never worried too much about it. The ads work.

As always, you'll want to double check that you've got everything the way you want before hitting "Submit campaign for review."

You've done it! You've written four ads. Nice job.

The report is reached by logging into AMS (Amazon Marketing Services: The place you go to run your campaigns). Below the orange "New campaign" button will be the reports.

At the top Amazon reminds us "Campaign metrics may take up to 3 days to appear and do not include Kindle Unlimited or Kindle Lending Library royalties generated by the ad."

To the right of the "New campaign" button is a search campaigns box. Moving father right is a gray button with a black download arrow on it. This is the button you'll use to download an Excel version of the data. Next to that button is a drop-down list "Results Per Page"

The gray bar below all of that has 13 headings. They are as follows:

1. Status: If it is green with the word Running, your campaign is active. You may click on the running button and toggle to "Paused" or terminate. The button may also say Ended or Rejected or if you did terminate the ad, it will say Terminate. Those are the status options.

   IMPORTANT: Be careful with this button. Once you TERMINATE, you can't undo it. It would be horrible to accidentally cancel your most productive ad.

2. Campaign Name: This is the name you chose for your ad when you set it up. This is why I suggested picking something that told you to include a naming convention that tells you which book the ad is for so you can easily identify it.

3. Type: It's either Product Display or Sponsored Product.

4. Start Date

5. End Date: This will be blank if it is a Sponsored Product ad that you intend to run for an indeterminate period of time.

6. Budget: This is your budget set aside for the ad. If it's a Sponsored Product ad you'll notice that next to the number, in light gray, it indicates "Daily:". An example might be "Daily: $5.00"

7. Impressions: The number of impressions the ad has had. In other words, how many times has your ad has been served up.

8. Clicks: This is the number of clicks. You probably figured that one out on your own.

9. ACPC (average cost per click): Just because you bid 15 cents, it doesn't mean you'll necessarily need to pay that for every click. If nobody else is bidding, you might get some clicks at a bargain, though this doesn't happen often.

10. Spend: This is the total that the ad has spent thus far.

11. Est. Total Sales: This is the estimated gross revenue from sales.

IMPORTANT: This is NOT your 70% or 35%. It is the retail price of your book times the number of sales. If you have a boxed set at $9.99 and you've had two sales, that number will be $19.98. Of course, you've only earned 70% of that, or just under $14.00.

12. ACoS (Advertising Cost of Sales): This is the amount you've spent on a campaign divided by the total unit sales during the campaign dates.

Generally, because the reporting is delayed by up to 72 hours, seeing a number north of 70% doesn't cause me to panic right away. Still, it's something you should keep an eye on.

# Chapter Four: Conversions

## Converting the Clicks

If you've been in the Indie Publishing game for more than three weeks you've already read that quality editing and cover art are important. There is a third equally important area that doesn't get talked about much. It's an area that nearly everyone mostly ignores. That means knowing what to do will give you an edge over traditionally published books and even your Indie publishing buddies.

I speak of the description.

This is the most hated aspect of the Indie Publishing world. In a recent poll taken in my Mastering Amazon Ads: An Author's Guide Facebook group, the three choices were:

1. "I don't mind writing descriptions"

2. "It annoys me a little"

3. "I'd rather have an impacted wisdom tooth that was removed by an angry badger"

In the poll twenty-one people went with the angry badger, twenty-people didn't mind writing the description, and nineteen people were annoyed a little bit. That's 66% of the respondents in this highly unscientific poll that found the practice at least somewhat bothersome.

Because I was curious about traditionally published novels, I started looking up successful books to see if they used proper copywriting technique in the descriptions. Were the publishers doing their best to convert when someone stopped in to see if they might be interested in *To Kill a Mockingbird*, *The Bluest Eye*, or *Snow Crash*, and the answer was a resounding meh, not so much.

It seems that if you're in charge of selling the winner of the Pulitzer Prize (1961 Fiction – *To Kill a Mockingbird*), or are promoting an author who won the Nobel Prize in literature (1993 – Toni Morrison), or you've been tasked to sell the seminal work on virtual reality (my personal opinion about *Snow Crash*, but I'm biased because Neal Stephenson went to my high school), then you just don't worry too much about converting.

Here's the thing, though. If one thinks like an analyst and imagines the next one million people who happen upon any of those three books, then some of them will need to be hooked. Yes, having a Pulitzer Prize or Nobel Prize helps with sales but so does good copy.

Those three books are easily in my top twenty-five favorites of all time, and it saddens me that their descriptions are so incredibly average.

Now, in the interest of full-disclosure, my descriptions used to be even worse than those written by Traditional published books. In fact, I have one that is still, as of the writing of this chapter, the worst description of all time. I'm not kidding. It's dreadful.

In this chapter, we're going to look at one of my best descriptions, and I'm going to show you the horrible one, . That will come in a bit. First, let's consider a test I did on ad copy for a landing page I was using for some Facebook ads.

The point of the ad campaign was to build my reader list for my science fiction series, The Magellan Apocalypse. Just like with Amazon ads, it's important to have good ad copy to get people to click past the landing page and head on over to Amazon.

For this campaign, I created a set of eight landing pages. They were identical. I did this so that I could target specific age ranges and break the ad into genders. So, if a 28-year-old female clicked on the Facebook ad, then she went to a different page than the 62 year old male who clicked on the same ad but that was targeted to his age range and gender.

This method allows me to tag the people that sign up for my reader group (aka email list, but we never call it that because people are sick of joining email lists). The idea is that if I build a massive list, I'll be able to learn a bit about my readers from knowing their age range and gender. It also allowed me to test ad copy.

Initial Ad Copy:

> Join the Magellan Apocalypse
> Reader Group and get the first
> Ebook in the series for FREE

*"Great candidate for the next space-based mini-series! A rollicking good series"* – Dave

*"Brilliant Space Trilogy"* – Burt Y

*"Five Stars. I couldn't put it down."* - Jill

This was the copy used across all eight identical pages. It did NOT convert well. Over the week, I let the ad run before messing with the copy. I was converting a lowly 1:9 people who clicked. The copy needed to be better. (Note: the ":" is read as "in.")

Let's begin with why this copy failed.

The call to action was at the beginning and was weak. The start of the copy should always be a hook.

One might argue that the hook is the free offer, but there are too many free books available for that to be special in this day and age. If Mark Twain had run this on Facetome, a free offer would have been a novel approach, pun intended.

The second problem was that after the hook should come another hook to lead the person through the copy. Thirdly, the order of the quotes isn't good. I'll talk more about this later. Suffice it to say, this ad copy was less than ideal.

Of course, being an optimist, by setting the bar so low I had a much easier time improving.

The second attempt was a little better.

Second Version:

This new post-apocalyptic space opera will keep you turning the pages.

If you like aliens, a struggle for survival, and a little bit of snark, then you'll enjoy this series.

Praise for The Magellan Apocalypse:

*"A rollicking good series. Greatly enjoyed this story. Hints of Battlestar Galactica but BIGGER. Is about a group of friends managing to survive in an interstellar colonization ship of incredible size. Lots of ship to explore and many hair-raising adventures doing it. I could definitely see this being turned into a mini-series."* – Dave M

*"Magellan Apocalypse is a fantastic novel about a battle to recapture a generation ship after a disaster. The writing is excellent and the story is interesting and exciting. The characters are well developed and the tech is very realistic. I couldn't put it down. Great sci fi!"* – Burt Y

*"Great series - fast paced. Pulls you quickly into the main characters. Was disappointed when I reached the end of book 3 - there wasn't any more to read!"* – G

Your New Favorite Space Opera

Get the First Novel in the series for FREE

\*\*\*\*\*\*

This is an improvement though only by a little. The opening line is too long. One wants the reader to be able to take it all in while they're skimming the copy, something we all do before reading.

The second line is better but I still didn't get the order of the quotes right in the "Praise for..." section. The first one should be the shortest so the reader is more likely to actually read it.

As for the end of this copy, it is much improved as this is where the call to action belongs.

It converted at about 1:7, which was an improvement but a long way from where I wanted.

The next step was to try some ad copy that was gender specific. I wanted to know if the reader's gender mattered with regard to the copy.

Third Version (Done with the screen split into two columns):

| Do you miss Firefly? | |
|---|---|
| | |

Did you enjoy the snarky banter mixed with the genuine attraction between characters?

Meet Fristion Nash, a fighter pilot who's snarky, charming, and great in a fight... but will he save the day?

No.

Now, meet Sasha.

Her specialty is keeping Nash from getting killed. Sasha likes Nash—he's rather handsome, thinks he's a bad ass, and is under the impression that he's the hero...

She thinks it's adorable.

In their world, though, two heroes may not be enough...

Join the Magellan Apocalypse Reader Group and get the first ebook in the series for FREE.

*"Great candidate for the next space-based mini-series!" "A rollicking good series" - Dave*

*"Brilliant Space Trilogy" - Burt Y*

*"Five Stars" "I love this story! Couldn't put it down!" - Jill*

The Magellan, a colonist class ship the size of a small country, is in trouble.

Come along on an adventure that begins with *The Magellan Apocalypse: Map Runners*, and discover your new favorite post-apocalyptic space opera...
...and hopefully fill the hole left by Firefly.

******

This is the copy I wrote for the female readers. It worked. The conversion immediately improved to 1:3. It has stayed there ever since.

I then wrote a male centric bit of copy and the same thing happened.

On the male centric copy, I only put it on three of the four landing pages because I wanted to test one more thing. I put the copy targeted at women on this fourth page.

Would it matter?

Do guys really care if the main character is a strong

woman who kicks ass?

The answer is yes. We (guys) are a sad, pathetic, insecure bunch, who can't handle strong women. The results made me weep. Sixty-two men clicked on the page and none of them signed up for the reader's group. Yes, zero for sixty-two!

Let's look at the copy. It starts with "Do you miss Firefly?"

That's a good hook because everyone misses Firefly, so the answer is always yes. If you've seen the series and subsequent movie and are not filled with a profound sadness that it all came to an end, then you're not human. Nope, you're some sort of artificial life form that has no idea you were made in a factory in another part of the galaxy.

So, in short, better hook.

The reader will have answered "yes" and this will make them want to read the next line. What's waiting for them? Another hook and then the quick answer to the question, an unexpected "No."

Now, hopefully the reader gets a feel for the humor in the series and wants to continue on.

This is the point where we introduce Sasha in all her bad assness. How many women can relate to letting their guy think he was in charge? Answer: All of them.

This is copy designed to hook women and each bit moves her down the copy. Also, notice how I used bold to make certain words stand out. This is to help with the initial scan so that the reader will be more likely to go back to the beginning and read our hook.

I learned a great deal from this experiment. The results were encouraging and the copy got me to a conversion that made me happy. It also reinforced the importance of taking copywriting (both the words and the layout) seriously.

## Optimizing Your Description

Let's start by looking at the worst description in the history of Amazon. Ironically, it's for *The Magellan Apocalypse (Books 1 – 3)* boxed set. Please note that, even though I discovered the importance of copywriting almost eight months ago, somehow, I let the description for my boxed set go unchanged.

I made the discovery about a week ago and decided to leave it until now so I could write about it in this book. Are you ready? It's really bad. If you're squeamish, you may want to skip the next part as the level of incompetency in this copy is sickening.

\*\*\*\*\*\*

The complete first trilogy of *The Magellan Apocalypse* series.
Includes: Book 1, Map Runners, Book 2, Asin's Hope, and Book 3, Red Swarm.

\*\*\*\*\*\*

Yes, that's it.

I don't think I need to do a thorough analysis of why this is sucky. At the time I put the book up for sale I just couldn't be bothered. The voice in my head, which is often a lying jerk, told me we'd come back to it later and do a proper job. Technically, the voice was right, but it didn't mention anything about waiting eight months.

Here is an important point. This horrible description converts at 1:35. It's easily my worst performing copy. The reason I didn't notice it is because at $8.99 my margin is good, and my Product Display – Interest ads at eight cent clicks were still returning a massive ROI.

The lesson is, don't assume because something is going well that you haven't messed it up completely and are leaving a huge pile of money on the table. Please, read that last sentence again, and if it would help, get your loved one to have it tattooed on their bicep.

The answer to the question, "Have you tried testing…" is never, "No, the way I'm doing now is really good so why bother?" Yes, even if you're getting 300% ROI, don't assume it's good. Perhaps you could be getting two or three times that.

Even if you're completely happy with your results and don't need any more money, consider this, if you did improve your results you could take that extra cash you didn't need and donate it to starving children in faraway lands.

In short, always be striving for improvement or you'll be killing babies. Don't kill babies.

So, let's take a look at the copy for book one in the series.

******

A new world waited for the Magellan. A new alien race waited, too.

When a massive attack leaves the Magellan crippled en route, there are more questions than answers. Nash leads the Map Runners. Their job, survey and survive.

On a ship that's got thousands of cubic miles to explore, with danger lurking behind every turn, and a commanding officer that wants Nash dead, his next run may be his last.

If you like post-apocalyptic space opera, then this is the series for you.

\*\*\*\*\*\*

Is this copy that I'd give an A?

It is not.

As I mentioned, the quotes need to be in reverse order or at the very least, the third one moved to the top.

The first line isn't perfect either. It would be better if I had put the second sentence on its own line.

A new world waited for the Magellan.

A new alien race waited, too.

It's much easier to get the reader to move from one short part to the next.

The rest of the copy is fair, though there should be a call to action at the end. As such, when grading this, I can only give it a B, and that's only because this ad copy has been sucking up to me all semester and bringing me apples daily.

But what of the results?

This copy converts at a range of 1:8 to 1:11. That's a pretty decent conversion, though not as good as the next example. Remember, each time we make a change to improve the conversion, our return on investment improves because we don't have to pay for as many clicks to get a result.

## Evolution of a Description

When I hit publish on the first book in my satire series, *Underwood, Scotch, and Wry*, my description certainly ended up different than how it began.

Original Description for *Underwood, Scotch, and Wry*:

*****

*Underwood, Scotch, and Wry* is a humorous look at social media through the eyes of a Luddite college professor.

Arthur enjoys drink, the company of his female TAs, and generally being a pain in the butt for the dean of the

English department. He has tenure. He hates computers.

The dean hates him.

Watch as Arthur and the dean engage in an angst filled battle to end (or save) his job. This humorous fiction will keep you turning the pages. If you like social media, blogging, and mockery, you'll enjoy my first satire novel *Underwood, Scotch, and Wry.*

\*\*\*\*\*

It looks pretty much like all the descriptions out there. Don't try to do what everyone else is doing in your genre because most of them are doing it wrong. This includes the traditional publishers.

The next thing I did was add the following bit to the top.

> It should be noted that I no longer use the Praise For... at the top of my descriptions because it is against Amazon's Terms of Service. I sort of knew this but ignored it for a long time. Some helpful author friends of mine point out that I was in violation and after much consideration realized it wasn't worth the risk.

> That being said, I leave it in here as an example of how a single change can impact conversion.

I do NOT recommend doing this in your descriptions moving forward.

Here is the section from the TOS.

*"The inclusion of any of the following information in detail page titles, descriptions, bullet points, or images is prohibited:*

*Pornographic, obscene, or offensive content.*

*Phone numbers, physical mail addresses, email addresses, or website URLs.*

*Availability, price, condition, alternative ordering information (such as links to other websites for placing orders), or alternative shipping offers (such as free shipping).*

*Spoilers regarding Books, Music, Video, or DVD (BMVD) listings (information that reveals plot elements crucial to the suspense, mystery, or surprise ending of a story).*

*Reviews, quotes, or testimonials.*

*Solicitations for positive customer reviews.*

*Advertisements, promotional material, or watermarks on images, photos, or videos.*

*Time-sensitive information (i.e., dates of promotional tours, seminars, lectures, etc.)."*

******

Praise for US&W:

"Absolutely fabulous wit and dialogue." – M.W.
"Thoroughly enjoyed this book. Being a former "non-computer nerd" there was much to make me laugh! I may even try Twitter now! – Debbie J. W.
"With a salute to social media, the author presents a loveable scoundrel who entertains one page after page. Nicely done." –H. R.

\*\*\*\*\*\*

The original description converted at 1:20 – 1:30.

The addition of this bit improved my page reads by 35% immediately.

The following description improved my conversion rate to 1:6 – 1:10.

\*\*\*\*\*\*

Praise for *Underwood, Scotch, and Wry*:

*"Absolutely fabulous wit and dialogue." – M.W.*
*"Thoroughly enjoyed this book. Being a former "non-computer nerd" there was much to make me laugh! I may even try Twitter now! – Debbie J. W.*
*"With a salute to social media, the author presents a lovable scoundrel who entertains one page after page. Nicely done." –*

*H. R.*

## Not Every Hero is Heroic

Arthur Byrne is a lot of things…bitter, ambivalent, angst ridden, snarky, and more than anything…he's a writer who can't write anymore. So, naturally, he became a professor.

A life in academia has allowed Arthur to hone his drinking skills, spend time with age-inappropriate teaching assistants, and avoid the demons that silenced his Underwood many years before.

He might describe himself as an anti-hero, if he weren't so against the term.

*Underwood, Scotch, and Wry* is a satirical look at social media and modern technology through the eyes of a Luddite college professor whose days at Beckerston College are numbered.

The Dean wants him gone.

The President wants him gone.

Arthur wants to be left alone.

Can a group of Teaching Assistants led by Wen Hu, a

twenty-eight-year old suffering from unbridled optimism, save Arthur from dismissal…and himself?

Pick up this page turner today!

Author Interview:

You didn't start out writing satire fiction. What made you dip your toes into this genre?

You're right, I began writing the Henry Wood series and then penned *A Touch To Die For*. I had always been snarky on my blog and one day I got a tweet from a reader who wanted to know why I didn't write humor and satire. I replied that I didn't know why and would start that day. And I did.

How did you choose to write a satire about social media?

I had written a number of blog posts for PR bloggers and they were always humorous looks at social media. Those posts were well received, so it was a natural place to begin. *Underwood, Scotch, and Wry* is supposed to be both entertaining and educational for those who might not know much about social media. I've heard from a number of people that say they really liked the underlying education throughout.

Who would enjoy this novel?

People who regularly use the word snark will appreciate Arthur Byrne.

Read *Underwood, Scotch, and Wry* for FREE with your Kindle Unlimited subscription and look for it under Humor and Entertainment.

\*\*\*\*\*\*

This is my favorite and best performing bit of copy I've used in descriptions. I spent the most time on it and truly considered every word, the cadence, the hooks, and the points that are supposed to be funny.

Admittedly, this is also my book with the most reviews (530 plus as of this writing), which is more social proof that of *The Magellan Apocalypse: Map Runners* (26 reviews) has. This may be part of the reason for a better conversion. Also, US&W has a better rating, 4.3 to 4.0. It's a better book.

Regardless, this version is a nice example of what I go for when writing descriptions now. The author interview at the end is there merely to give a bit more information in a SEO friendly way.

IMPORTANT:

This chapter is one of the most crucial of the

book. If you don't take the time to review and improve your book's description, then you're giving your precious creation a handicap. We spend a lot of time writing our novels and it only makes sense to give a little effort in creating the right first impressions, or second if one is counting the cover art, which one should.

Furthermore, the rest of the book is about advertising and clicks. You pay for the clicks. You WANT them to convert as frequently as possible.

A top-quality description is key.

Now, go review your description and ask the following questions:

1. Is there a hook that grabs the reader with just the briefest of glances?

2. Are the paragraphs written as good copy, short and to the point? Good.

3. Or are they more like the writing inside the book, full of lovely prose? Bad.

4. Is there a call to action?

# Chapter Five: Setting Expectations

Amazon advertising is both simple and challenging. Writing an advertisement can take only a couple of minutes. Building a series of ads and maintaining them so that one is generating "quit your day job" sort of money is the challenge.

The single most difficult aspect of making money with AMS ads is figuring out how to spend more money. What I mean by that is once you've found the sweet spot with the bid and sales have started to come in profitably, you'll want to increase how much you're spending. If you spend a dollar and get two dollars back, you'll be dying to know how to spend $50.00 or $500.00. It's not that easy to scale.

Perhaps the most frustrating thing about the ads is when a great campaign suddenly stops getting any impressions. We will look at this in detail and give some strategies to help avoid days without spend.

We will also look at how one tracks their ads to determine the ROI.

The other challenge is that the market changes. This impacts the tried and true methods we get used to and makes us find new solutions. It can be easy to panic when months of wonderful sales results come screeching to a halt. The trick is to have solid data and understanding of the current state of Amazon ads and adjust accordingly. I'll give an example later.

I'll also be sharing some data with you from my own ads as examples. I write across six genres: Mystery, YA, Science Fiction, Satire/Humor, Thriller, and non-fiction. Each of these markets is different. Of course, there are many other genres and hopefully after seeing these examples you'll find that your genre has similarities with one of the six mentioned.

We'll be investigating the different types of ads and explain how one tells if an ad is performing well, beyond just the ROI.

Did the beginning of the chapter sound like another "Introduction"?

Well, it was. It may not be the last.

Reality Check Letter to Readers:

Dear Author Friends,

I wanted to write a few things at this point because I know what's coming. In short, frustration.

You may wonder how I know this. Well, there is a bit of back story here and I beg you to read it.

In late February 2017, I was under the mistaken impression that had finished writing Mastering Amazon Ads: An Author's Guide. I set up a beta group on Facebook to get feedback. I built a tool in Excel to help them with analysis. And then the questions started. This is where I learned about what I'd like to call the Teacher's Paradox.

After about a month of interacting with the folks in the group, answering questions, and writing chapters I didn't know the book needed, people started to get frustrated. This stressed me out. More than anything I wanted my book to help people succeed. That's not hyperbole, I thought about nothing else but getting their ads to succeed.

My initial writing, it turned out, went way too far into the weeds. People wanted simple steps to learn this process. Presumably you've read through three chapters and been given easy instructions to learn how to begin.

At the point where people were getting frustrated they had only read as much as you have now. I was writing and rewriting all in an attempt to make things as easy as possible.

That's where the paradox begins.

In an attempt to make the instructions simple to follow, my writing gave the impression that earning five figures per month was just a matter of putting up a few ads (easy as Sunday morning).

It is NOT easy to make piles of money with ads.

So perhaps I should have written in more detail about the inner workings and what it takes?.

No, that doesn't work either because people stopped reading or skipped over complex explanations. I wrote them a letter (Yes, this is a letter within a letter)

******

Dear Beta Readers,

Many of you have gotten frustrated.

It's my fault.

I've not set expectations correctly.

There have been many instances where I've written that it takes a lot of work and testing. The problem is, I've not accounted for differing interpretations of what that might mean.

The Dilemma:

How do I present the subject in a way that is easiest for people to understand?

This has been my challenge since day one of this group. It became clear that most people wanted clear and easy instructions. Do this and then do that. They didn't want a lot of extra commentary.

We started with a section on how to set up ads. From there I've added additional chapters to ease people along the way. I've avoided going into too much detail.

The problem is, by doing this, I made it easier to understand and simultaneously gave the impression that this was easy.

It's not.

Okay, if you don't like reading long detailed posts, then perhaps this group isn't for you, because the only way I can think to get everyone on the same page is by explaining a few things...in GREAT detail so there isn't any confusion.

I've avoided going into my history too much, but if one understood how I got here, it might help with setting expectations.

Revenue by year:
2010 – 2012 = Less than $1,000
2013 = $5,000
2014 = $10,000
2015 = $33,000
2016 = $107,000

I'm not going to talk about how many books and all the details that went into each year. I did, however, throughout that entire time, devote a lot of my energy toward analysis.

Do you know the average number of downloads

on a BookBub free promotion? (or any of your promotions, for that matter?)

Do you know the rate of download per minute?

Do you know the best rate of download per minute the first hour after the email blast?

My best ever is 193 downloads per minute.

The point is not the data. The point is the work that goes into knowing that sort of data. When I run a BookBub promotion, I take a reading of the downloads from the moment the email blast goes out. I do this every 15 minutes for the next 20 hours.

Read that again.

I take a reading every 15 minutes for 20 straight hours and have done that for a dozen BookBub ads.

This is how I approach data.

Raise your hand if you're all of a sudden losing interest in the group, Amazon Ads, data, and analysis?

This is why I've eased into things. The realities are that if you want to follow the path I've taken to success, it requires work.

Let's be clear. I mean hours and hours every single week.

If you don't put in that time, you know what happens?

Your ad spend drops, your Cost Per Click increases (because you're not testing to find the absolute optimal bid) and your ROI goes down.

MY CURRENT ADS
Number: 88 ads across 5 books.

Distribution: 53 Keyword ads (only 8 of them are delivering more than 1,000 impressions per day)

35 Product Display ads (9 of them are delivering more than 1,000 impressions per day)

Yesterday's spend: $42.44

Yesterday's Budget: $46,130.00

My current ROI across everything is 252%.

Analysis of my Results:

Absolutely Horrible!

Yes, you read that correctly. Please understand that the next bit you are going to read is NOT a complaint, but an analysis of why my numbers are so awful (compared to before I started the group)

The group was started February 23rd, 2017. About a week later I started putting up stuff like the tool and some chapters.

All of my time has been spent on this group. I've been LOVING It. Most days I spend 12 hours and I do that seven days per week.

I have NOT been spending time on my ads. I have NOT been doing ANY analysis unless it was to write a chapter for the book.

I have NOT been doing testing, except as it pertains to trying to answer group questions or theories for the book.

Because I have not been doing the work required (which is a lot), my numbers are WAY down.

Before the AMS Facebook group: 35 sales per day

and 25,000 page reads.

Currently: 15 sales per day and 10,000 page reads.

All across the board my numbers have tanked. Why? Because I'm not working on my ads and doing the analysis.

It bears repeating. This is NOT complaining. I don't care that my numbers are down. The work that I'm doing in this group is FAR more important. And you know what? When I get the book out, I'll go right back to what I was doing before and the numbers will climb.

They will climb when I can again devote several hours per day to the ads.

I've had periods of 70 - 100 sales per day when the ad mix was right and everything fell into place.

My point, just so we're clear, is that the only way to succeed with Amazon ads is to spend a lot of time working on them.

The Problem:

What I need to teach YOU, the lab members, in

order to try to make a living the way I've done it. (Note: There are many ways to succeed in this business. This group is about how I've done it with Amazon ads. That's why we're here.)

1. To have an above average Excel competency
2. How to set up and use the tool
3. How to do data analysis
4. How to do math
5. How to do copywriting

Let's look at each one of these:

1) Excel Competency - You need to be able to use Excel to manage your data and know how to do it effectively.

I have been using Excel since before Excel existed. Yes, it used to be called Lotus 1-2-3. My father got version 1.0 on a HP laptop that was their FIRST laptop. I think this was in 1979 and Lotus 1-2-3 was hard coded in.

My Excel skills have been a major part of my analysis and success.

Do you need to be an Excel wizard?

No.

Do you need to know how to manipulate data, sort it, build formulas to do calculations on your own, and also know the time saving short cuts so you don't spend all day on the tasks?

Yes.

2) How to set up the tool.

1. This has been the biggest challenge. I'm trying to design a tool that all of you can use. It seems that about 80% of the people in the group have Macs.
2. If 100% had PCs, then I could have one single sheet where you pasted your daily data in (regardless of the source) and hit a button, and the workbook would put all of the data where it belongs.

I could write code that would allow the reports to present the data for any length of time and it wouldn't be pulling from formulas (which slows performance). It would be doing the calculations from the raw data.

At GEICO I built a tool that had over 200 pages of FB code alone to run it and the reporting provide a possible 141,000 unique pages of data.

I would be able to have dozens of more detailed reports analyzing your data in ways you can't even imagine.

But, that's not reality.

Please note, this isn't a bash on Macs. I have a Macbook Air, two iPads, and an iPhone. It is simply a fact that I've spent seven years as a data analyst learning VB coding and how it could be used in Excel to create massively complex (and efficient running) programs for PCs. And Macs won't run them.

This has been a horrible constraint on me for trying to help you.

As such, the tool is much more limited than I would like because most people have Macs. This is fine and I'm doing my best to accommodate.

3) How to do data analysis.

I've barely touched on analysis.

This means you've not been taught one of the key components to success for Amazon ads.

This will be the hardest part of the mission of this

group because some people don't even want to think about analysis.

Not only do I need to teach analysis, I need to figure out how to teach it in a way that makes a person who HATES the idea of staring at data want to do it.

This is no small feat.

Did I mention I had $107,000 in revenue last year?

Oh, and that I do this full-time.

And if I want to do something else on any given day, I can, because I don't have to go to a job.

Being a full-time author is freaking AWESOME!

I hope that the awesomeness of the life of a full-time author will be enough to convince those who don't want to learn about data that it's worth it.

4) How to do math.

Yes, you'll need to do math.

Do you remember when you asked your teacher,

"When will I ever use algebra in my life?"

Did they respond, "When you decide you want to be an author?"

Because, it turns out, that was the actual answer.

It's fine that some of you hate math. I'm not judging. But, in order for me to succeed in helping you make money using Amazon Ads, I'll need to train the part of your brain that handles things like algebra.

Again, no small task.

I'm happy to try.

5) How to do copywriting.

I'm still learning this art. If I weren't running this group, I'd probably be reading tons of copywriting books.

You need to understand how copywriting works because it is a KEY element in conversions.

Setting Expectations:

It took me three months of testing to get to where

I was seeing real results. It took another three months to get to $7,000 per month so I could quit my day job.

None of that time was spent learning Excel or How to Use the Tool (I built an earlier version that was VASTLY more complex long before I ever ran an AMS ad). I had seven years of data analysis experience and a degree in Economics, which is basically high-level algebra, so steps three and four were covered. I didn't, however, learn copywriting until September 2016.

The point is, it took me half a year to get it dialed in and I already had most of the tools (education wise) to figure this stuff out.

The expectation that many in the group have (in part because of my failure to write this post back in February) is that this would take a handful of ads and a few weeks to get going.

This is not the case, and I'm sorry that you've not understood.

Hurdles:

1) Learning the areas mentioned above that you don't fully grasp. It will take time.

2) Books - I had seven titles when I started AMS ads. I now have 14 and 2 boxed sets.

3) Time - Are you spending 40 - 60 hours per week on this business like I was back when I started AMS ads?

No?

You're feeding and clothing children. You're working a day job. You're spending time with friends.

That's fine. Those are all important things, but when I said I figured all of this out in six months, I did this while only working two days per week, I don't have children, and I went out and did things with friends one time over that six months.

Should you give up if you can't devote more than a few hours per week?

No! 100% No!!!!

This business doesn't have a shot clock. You are allowed to go at your own pace. You are NOT allowed to compare your results to someone who is working 10x as many hours as you and think you're a failure because your results are worse than theirs.

The human life expectancy is growing by 5 hours per day according to Steven Kotler in his new book *Stealing Fire*.

This is a long journey.

Again, I'm sorry I wasn't clear.

I hope you will continue to stay in the group, but if you want to leave, I won't hold it against you.

\*\*\*\*\*\*

That letter got great responses from the group.

One reply that I really liked was from Anil Polton, who wrote, "Great post and a shock reality check!!! Thank you Brian!"

That's what I was going for and hopefully, if you've not tossed the book (or your Kindle) aside, you'll be ready to move forward.

Here's how to proceed from here:

1. Understand that there is much to learn and it is worth taking your time to read one chapter at a time with a break before you move on to the next. All we've

covered thus far is the "how" one makes an ad. We've not gotten into strategy for building a successful ad portfolio.

2. Reread Chapter 3. The copywriting stuff and your description are more important than I can accurately describe given the limits in our language. We need a word for "More important than ordering a side of bacon with breakfast." Seriously, it's THAT important.

3. Don't panic. There are many times you'll want to freak out over your click-through rate, or your ACoS number, or which ad is really performing the best. This is a long game. Even if you do make mistakes they just don't matter much over the next 30 years of your book sales.

4. This is going to take time to learn and master. Plan on six months to a year.

5. If you're feeling dread at all you've just read, remember, it's worth it to be a full-time author.

One last note. I've struggled to figure out the order that I feed you this information. It's definitely a which came first, the chicken or the egg sandwich sort of dilemma. And all I can say is I've put a lot of thought into the chapter order. People learn different ways and perhaps it would be best to think of each individual chapter as its own volume. After you've finished the book you can go back and reference the areas that will help you the most.

# Chapter Six: The Horrible Story

So, you've run four ads. You're excited. Let me tell you how sometimes the wonderful parade of sales can be rained on by changing circumstances.

On January 4, 2016 Amazon sent out a letter encouraging authors to use their AMS service. Ugh, I thought. This is going to mean a flood of new users. I had just come off my best month and was looking forward to continued growth. It all stopped on that cold January morning.

I knew how much of a challenge it was to make a profit with Amazon ads. I also knew that the minimum budget was $100.00. My analyst brain spent an afternoon thinking about how things might play out.

Here was my reasoning. I hope you'll do a similar thought exercise the first time that something drastic happens to impact your sales.

At the time, the suggested bid was .29 - .47 (or thereabouts). Prior to that email I had read dozens of blog posts and forum posts from other authors complaining about how it was impossible to make money using Amazon ads. It seemed that one hundred percent believed it couldn't be done.

What I knew that none of those writers seemed to have discovered was that, as I mentioned, the "suggested bid" was too high. In almost every case they tested the waters with a single ad, using the lower end of the suggested bid, and then they watched as the clicks burned through a big chunk of their $100 budget and resulted in few sales. Across the board they lost money.

The second point was that the default date range for an ad was 30 days (now it's 60).

I told a couple of authors who I was coaching on their own ads that I didn't think it was the end of the world. I predicted that our impressions would be almost non-existent for a month and then they would miraculously come back to life.

On February 4, 2016 my ads started getting traction again. It wasn't back to where it had been overnight but it steadily improved.

The reasoning behind my correct prediction was that most people who tried the AMS system would run their first ad with the suggested bid and get crushed. It would take a month for them to see the results and they'd give up. That's exactly what happened.

So, now AMS has been opened up to the world. That means Indie authors who are not exclusive can run ads. Did I see my impressions plummet again?

Yes.

Do I think that in a month it will go back to the good old days? No, not this time.

The big difference is that the suggested bid is .15 - .25 and if a book has a high enough margin, great ad copy, and a great cover, then it is VERY possible to do quite well.

The bottom line is it means that we all need to bring our A-game. That means that we need to run lots of ads, do lots of tests, and most of all pay attention to the data.

Don't worry. I've got this. And I'm going to show you how to build a consistent set of ads and show you how to rotate to maximize your return.

# Chapter Seven: Watching Impressions

## Watching Impressions

It can be easy to set up an ad and forget it. When you find one that works, the assumption is that it will keep working for a long time. This is not the case. In the two years I've been doing this I've seen periods where ads will deliver consistent impressions measuring in the thousands to tens of thousands per day for three straight weeks.

I once had a group of a couple ads that delivered 600,000 - 800,000 impressions per day for a solid week. That was a very good week. The problem is that the ads will quickly drop to nothing (I define nothing as less than a few hundred impressions in a day.)

It seems that if one ad runs well for 7-10 days that all of my ads will only run well for that same length of time. If it is three weeks, then they will all do well for three weeks.

Another aspect to keep an eye on is when an ad begins to generate impressions. By this, I mean you may have an ad get approved and the next day it has 54 impressions. That is NOT an ad that I consider to be running. When the ad suddenly goes to 5,000 impressions in a single day, then you can be sure it is running. At this point, if you've been paying attention and know how long an ad will typically run, you'll be prepared for when it stops.

This brings me to the next thing to watch for and that's how long it takes for an advert to turn on. This also seems to vary over time. Also, when you're running a lot of ads, you'll find some of them never turn on. This is especially true if you're doing testing to find out the minimum bid you can use to maximize your profitability.

You need to always know how long ads take to start and how long they will run.

Example:

Let's say you have found success with a Product Display - Interest ad. Imagine that it has taken about five days for most of your ads to turn on, and they run for seven days.

That means that if you write a new ad today, it will start to generate impressions in five days, but in twelve days it will stop. So, to avoid a drop off, plan on writing a replacement in seven days.

This is why it's important to stay on top of your impressions because they are the clue as to what's happening with regards to duration of delivering impressions.

I should mention that in most cases when an ad stops running it won't start up again. That being said, sometimes they will flicker to life a day or two before the end of the date range and you'll get a nice spike. For that reasons, even when an ad appears to be dead, I still leave it on.

The only time I pause or terminate an ad is when it's failing miserably.

## Reporting Delays

This is an important aspect to understand. Amazon tells us that our ads may not report the true impressions, clicks, spend, and sales right away. This is absolutely true. I've noticed that sales seem to have the longest delay. The most obvious indication that there is lag in reporting is when an ad has been terminated or reached the end of its date range and is in "Ended" status and the next day there are more impressions, clicks, spend, and sales. Always be watching your data, and you'll start to have an understanding of how the delay impacts your results.

Another strange quirk about the AMS system at present is that sometimes the accumulation of the spend (charging for clicks) is delayed on the billing history.

The Billing History link/tab is to the right of the Advertising Campaigns at the top of the page. Once you start running a lot of ads, you'll sometimes see an AMS invoice marked paid in full for a date of 1/19/2017, which is fine. You're happy to pay for the ads that are making you money.

Then you might notice that the "accumulating" ad says the current invoice is from 1/11/2017, which looks like they're double billing because you've already paid in full up through the 19th.

I don't know officially why the invoices look back dated but I suspect it's just because of the aforementioned delays. It's not a big deal. Don't panic.

I keep a really close eye on my ads and the amount I'm actually being billed matches up with the spend that my ads have reported. That being said, I do check those numbers often just to be safe.

I know it seems like I'm digging really deep into the weeds here, but the hope is to give you the future advertiser, enough of an understanding to prosper. The whole back dating thing might never be a detail that 90% of you notice, but if you know it's not something to worry about, if that day comes, there's a much less of a chance of a major cardiac event.

# Chapter Eight: Understanding

# Budgets and Scaling

If you've had any experience in running Facebook ads, you know that one of the biggest warning to new advertisers from those in the know is to be careful with your budget. Facebook is really good at taking your money.

Amazon, at present, is not.

It isn't, I imagine that they don't want to take your money. And truth be told, I've never put an ad up with a crazy bid of .30 per click, but if you use conservative bidding, you'll not need to fear a massive spend.

In fact, once you get good at running profitable ads, you'll be more concerned about NOT spending a ton.

As you know, I suggested a really small budget in the ads we ran earlier. I do NOT follow that advice.

Understanding Budget: This is perhaps the most important aspect of the book!

1. Your fears: Right now you don't have tons of money in the bank. You're afraid of making a mistake and all of your money disappearing. I get that.

2. Billing limits: Understand that Amazon will never let your bill reach more than about $510.

3. Declined Payment: If you have a debit card attached to pay for your bill and let's say you only have $282 in the account when Amazon tries to collect for the $510 that you owe, nothing terrible happens. They are unable to collect part of the money, so they simple pause all your ads. Okay, if your ads are crushing it, then it is a big deal, but the point is their system is like an automatic break.

To get the ads up and running again you'll simply need to go into the *Payment Settings* and replace the card. If it is a case that you only have one card, but you've just transferred money into the account so that the balance is now greater than the $510 that you owe, then just put in the same card again and hit update.

Amazon will then process the payment. It can take 3 - 12 hours for the payment to go through.

If your daily spend is a few bucks it's not a big deal. If you're spending $250.00 per day and that amount is driving $700 worth of sales, the paused ads will make you sad...very sad.

Okay, so now it's time to look deeper into the questions of budget. We are still in the MOST IMPORTANT section. In fact, I'd say this next story is worth the price of the book. It will change how you think about your ads.

I love data and I spend hours and hours just staring at the raw numbers. I'm a former data analyst and that's not uncommon behavior. We look for patterns that make us stop and ask questions.

I was at a point where my revenue had grown greatly but I couldn't seem to get my spend over $100 per day. Breaking through and increasing my spend was my quandary and I was trying to find a hint in the data.

At the time, I had run 131 different ads. For the first dozen, I had chosen a budget of $100 on Product Display ads. When it was clear they were working, I increased it to

$200. That's where I was at the day I made the 48% discovery.

I noticed that there wasn't a single ad that had spent over 48% of my "Budget." Not one single ad. It didn't matter if they were ones that had great CTR or not. None of them crossed the 48% threshold.

In fact, in the 650 plus ads I've run, there has only been one time an ad went over 48%, and it was my best ad ever at 55% of the budget.

This is the important part that I was talking about. When you're ready to increase your spending, the first thing you must do is increase the budget.

I've tested budgets of $400, $800, $1200, and $2000. I didn't see any benefit to going from $1200 to $2000, but I still occasionally try it.

Now, what this means, because we're telling Amazon they can run our ads as quickly as possible, that we're committing to them being able to spend $1200 on a single ad in a single day.

Does that frighten you?

It shouldn't. Let me explain.

As an example, let's say your ad is bidding .15 per click

(which is MORE than I typically bid, for the record). That would be 8,000 clicks in a single day. If your description is high quality copy writing, you have a professional cover, and enough reviews for reasonable social proof, then a reasonable conversion rate is between one in six and one in ten clicks.

At one in ten clicks, that's 800 sales or downloads. If the book is priced at $4.99, and if we imagine that half of the clicks are sales and half are free downloads in KU, then the revenue from sales is $1380. And the page read revenue, assuming 300 KENPC is going to be based upon 120,000 page reads.

But let's assume some portion of the readers don't finish the book and so it's only 50,000 page reads. At .005, that's another $2500.00.

If you could spend $1200 and get back $3880, you'd do that every day of the week.

But again, I've never seen them spend over 55% of a budget, and that was only once. I've looked at all of my *Prosperity for Author's* series co-author Honorée's ads, too, and it's the same.

And then there's the stop gap that you may not have enough money to cover the $1200.

But let's say your description didn't convert, even if it was 1:20, that's in the black. That being said, I wouldn't go crazy with the budget until you're sure that nearly ever ad you run will be profitable and you're in the habit of keeping eye on it.

As for me, my daily exposure is often between $40,000 - $80,000. At present, my spend is rarely over $100. My goal for over a year has been to try to have a $1000.00 spend day. My record is $350. Of course, I'm bidding at a level that will be profitable. I could bid much higher, say .30 per click and I'm sure I'd be able to crank up the daily spend. I would, however, NOT be profitable except in the case of my boxed sets.

# Chapter Nine: First Plan

First Plan

Right now you've learned a few things. You know how to run all four types of ads. You're aware of the importance of having a quality description to best optimize your conversions. And you've learned a bit about the importance of the budget on being able to increase your spend.

It's time to craft your first plan of attack.

We're going to start with a simple set of ads for one book.

1. Choose your book.

2. Write one Sponsored Product – Keyword ad and include at least 200 keywords or more if you're feeling frisky. Bid no more than .25 cents per

keyword at this time.

3. Write one Product Display – Product ad. Bid .10 on a list of 200 products (probably book titles from similar books)

4. Write five Product Display – Interest ads. Bid .08, .08, .10, .10, and .12 on the ads. Choose the same interests for all five ads. Write different ad copy for each ad.

That's a total of seven ads for one book.

What can you expect from those ads?

It can be hard to tell, but I would guess that it goes something like this. The keyword ad will start getting impressions first. When it's getting a few thousand impressions per day you'll start to get a few clicks. The more keywords you have included the large the number of impressions will be and the more clicks you'll get.

The Product Display – Product ad may get going next, but it will likely take longer than the keyword ad.

The group of five ads will take longer to get going. It may take them up to five weeks before anything happens. Some of the ads may not ever turn on. You may want to panic despite my repeated efforts to encourage you not to do so. Please don't.

The Product Display - Interest ads will require fewer impressions to get clicks. If you're getting several thousand impressions per day, you'll be getting 15 – 20 clicks from those ads compared to only 1 – 2 from the keyword ads. Also, you'll likely have a lower cost per click (CPC).

This is still the early stages of your development. The results are less important than gaining an understanding of the methodology to building a plan.

These ads may do fine for you or they may not do much of anything but I want you to set them and then let them run without doing any editing or changing of the bid.

I repeat. Don't change the bid to try to get the ads to work.

Do I need to say it a third time?

I don't recommend ever editing an ad to try to get it to perform better. Please always just write a new ad if there is something you want to test. Keeping the old ads untouched will give you better data to analyze. Also, because most people tend to error on the side of quickly increasing their bid, this original ad, when it does start working, may be the proof you need to avoid further panicking down the road.

Like the first chapter that told you how to run ads, this is just a very basic beginner plan. If you follow these steps before moving on to more complex ideas in the book, I believe you'll find them easier to understand.

# Chapter Ten: Rejection

Sometimes an ad gets rejected. Often it can be pretty easy to fix. One ad got rejected because a single word was in ALL CAPS. They don't like it if an ad starts with something other than a letter. The reviewers want complete sentences that are grammatically correct.

Here are a few of the issues they may cause an ad to be rejected:

1. Incomplete sentence

2. Grammar errors

3. All caps on a word

4. Too sexy or sexually suggestive cover art

5. Images of blood on the cover

6. Reviews with quotation marks around them

7. Multiple exclamation points!!! (See what I did there? I make myself giggle. I'm adorable.)

8. Use of ellipses

9. Mentioning the price

It's important to remember that the review process isn't an exact science.

> In my Facebook group, Mastering Amazon Ads: An Author's Guide - Beta, Brian Berni wrote, "One of my ads had the acronym 'BS' (as in bull ****). It got rejected once. Then, I re-submitted the ad and changed absolutely nothing, and it got approved."

> Robert Fear wrote, "I've only had one rejected because I used a 5* quote. Amazon said that it could not be relied on because the reviewer could change their star rating at any time." Robert went on to get the exact text of their reply, "The ad contains references to customer reviews or star ratings. As the star ratings on Amazon are dynamic and can change rapidly, the star rating in your ad may not be correct throughout your ad

campaign." Robert is nothing if not thorough.

H Claire Taylor said, "They're not huge on religious symbols on the cover or the word God. But you can wear them down on this. Believe me." (Personal Note: H Claire's Jessica Christ book series is brilliant satire.)

There are also times that they simply will reject a cover because the reviewer has made a mistake. In one ad, the reviewer rejected the ad for a spelling error. The problem was I had not misspelled the word "When." I had correctly spelled the first name of my 28-year-old Chinese-American character "Wen" Hu.

To resolve the issue, I wrote an email. It was passed on to someone else. I wrote at length about how it was a proper name and even gave some statistics about how many people, approximately, might have this name in China. Eventually, after much back and forth I got the ad approved.

There were two lessons from this experience. The first was that Amazon will work hard to correct issues if they are in the wrong. The second was that I'm an idiot.

I spent probably 30 minutes crafting emails and responses to get an ad approved that takes three minutes to write. A better use of my time would have been to simply rewrite the copy.

Although, I did feel a fair amount of satisfaction when it was finally sorted out in my favor. And the ad did get to run.

How did the ad end up doing?

I don't think it ever got any impressions. So, not great.

The point is that in the book business there are a lot of things to worry about, but rejected ads aren't one of them. If an ad gets rejected for something like cover art with blood, I'd not panic about that either. I'd just write another ad and keep trying. The next ad might not get rejected.

I could give examples of something that got rejected one time and not another, but this isn't really a subject worth beating to death.

You'll have some rejected ads. If it's easy to fix, then fix it, otherwise move along.

# Chapter Eleven: Intro to Analysis

Intro to Analysis

It's about to get fun up in here. I'm giddy.

This is the section of the book that is born from two years of staring at my numbers and asking the questions, "Why? And what if?"

Each day we need to look at our numbers and make decisions. Should I pause an ad? Should I run eight more Product Display – Interest ads for that book? Should I raise my bid? Is my advertising copy the best it could be? Am I losing money? Am I making money but could I be making more? Will a BLT for lunch be delicious and make me happy?

With the exception of the last question which is obviously yes in every case, we need to learn how to see patterns to make informed decisions. We need to be able to spot incongruent numbers that trigger a quest for more answers.

This is not a skill set that everyone has and it can take a while to develop. The wonderful thing about this chapter is that you'll be learning how I arrived at some of the assumptions I carry with me about how to read data and when to trust the data.

The last bit is worth repeating. One should always be on the lookout for data that are lying to you. Sometimes it is a case that you made a mistake in how you recorded your data. Other times the numbers on the AMS report may say one thing but need to be considered to be incomplete data and not used for decision making.

First let's look at an instance where I'm 99% sure the sales data are accurate on the AMS report and how I know it to be true.

1. Book: *Underwood, Scotch, and Wry*
2. Price Point: $4.99
3. Ad: Sponsored Product
4. Bid: .08
5. Daily Budget: $100.00

This ad barely ran. That's fine. It was a test and I run a lot of ads at low bids to see what happens. This is how I learn.

Though the ad is still live, it was started on 1/24/17 and only generated impressions for a few days. The impressions were 6,696 with 5 clicks. The average cost per click was .06.

As Amazon clearly states, it can take a while for the data to fully populate in the report. This ad did not generate impressions for many days in a row before it stopped completely. It showed zero sales for a while, too. Eventually, though, the sales totals did populate. Total sales revenue according to the AMS report was $24.97.

Let's analyze this ad.

First of all, with a price point of $4.99, and keeping in mind that the AMS report returns gross sales revenue (retail price) and not the 70% royalty that we authors earn, the $24.97 tells me that there were five sales. That being said, it does seem odd that it would be $24.97 and not $24.95. I can't explain the two cents difference. The fact that there is a difference, though, is worth noting. Anytime something seems off, always make a mental note to look for similar occurrences in the future. It may be a valuable piece of information.

Okay, the next thing to consider is do five sales represent all the sales this ad could have generated? I would never expect to get five sales from five clicks, I would expect to get one, maybe. However, with each click there is a possibility the reader clicking will want the book and buy. It may be unlikely to go five for five but it is possible.

Since there were only five sales and the report shows five sales it must be representative of all of the possible sales. There could not be six sales on five clicks.

This is why I'm 99% sure the number is accurate.

If this was a person's only data with regard to the AMS reporting then they would be feeling confident in its accuracy.

Now, let's look at another ad for the same book.

1. Book: *Underwood, Scotch, and Wry*
2. Price Point: $4.99
3. Ad: Product Display – Interest
4. Bid: .17
5. Lifetime Budget: $1200.00

There are several important things to consider during this analysis. The first is that as a general rule I will have 10 – 20 Product Display – Interest ads turned on for this book. At any given time there might be 3 – 12 of them generating impressions and clicks. My best week ever for this book was 15 ads all crushing it. For that whole week, the book was ranked between #520 and #980 overall.

This ad though was one of only two that were generating impressions and clicks on 3/27/17.

In this analysis, it's important to understand what was happening over the three days prior. The total number of clicks were as follows from 3/24 – 3/26: 4, 3, and 6. This book typically converts at about 1:6 - 10, so the expectation would be zero to one sale or download during that three-day span.

Obviously, with such low numbers a sale can come in that is unrelated to the ad. Don't let your inability to be able to swear on a stack of pancakes that your analysis is iron clad stop you from drawing reasonable conclusions. This is what I hope you learn.

What were the actual results over those three days from the AMS report? Both ads showed zero sales. Okay, what about KDP?

One sale per day. It should be noted there was a precipitous drop in page reads, which makes me think that those 13 clicks over that span didn't bring in any new KU downloads.

To review, it looks like those three days of one sale per day were driven by the ads. The total spend was $1.85.

I'm not going to calculate the ROI this time because it is unrelated to the point of this particular analysis.

Now, let's look at the five days from 3/27/17 to 3/31/17.

The impressions for those four days were as follows: 11, 11, 9, 10, 41 for a total of 82 clicks.

Most of the spend came from the ad in question. The daily spend was $1.87, $1.56, $1.53, $1.70, and $6.82.

A good habit to get into when analyzing data is to try to predict your results before looking up the answer. I would predict that 82 impressions would yield around 14 sales.

Of course, as we know from the first example one can get on a hot streak and it is just as likely that one might get a point where 20 people will click and zero will buy.

The number we're looking for is going to be in the neighborhood of 14.

How many sales would you guess the AMS report is showing?

There have been zero additional sales added to the report.

Well, that doesn't sound good at all. This is where one needs to look for more information. We know that the previous three days saw the book only get one sale per day. It was NOT selling like a stack of hot cakes. (Yes, this chapter is brought to you by breakfast…one of the top five most important meals of the day.)

The daily unit sales according to KDP were 4, 3, 4, 4, 8. I know some of you are not fans of math but I'm guessing that you can see the difference between the daily sales above and the AMS reported sales of 0, 0, 0, 0, 0.

There is much more going on here than simply verifying that the ads in question are driving sales. We are also going to explore a phenomenon where it seems like all ads start out great and then get much worse with regards to their profitability.

Can you guess what is going on here with this ad?
First of all, the reporting is slow. This means that the daily spend numbers, click and impressions on the 27th are likely understated. Each of the days in this example may actually have more impressions, clicks, and spend than we know.

How do I know this?

First of all, the number of sales is 23 not 14. Over years of practice I've gotten really good at estimating things of this nature. I'm not usually off by 64%.

Also, I have two years' worth of doing this sort of analysis, so I can look at just these numbers and know something isn't adding up. If I take 88 clicks and divide it by 23 sales (assumes zero KU downloads which on 88 clicks is highly unlikely. I'd estimate another 15 or so people downloaded the book) we get the number 3.82 or more accurately a conversion rate of 1:3.82 which is quite a bit better than 1:6 - 10. The 1:6 - 10number is based upon over a half years' worth of data since I changed my description.

Another concept to understand is that a larger length of time gives more accurate data because random occurrences smooth out over time.

With the first example, I could believe that I got lucky and had five sales in a row.

Now, if we factor in what I know of KU, the number gets even better (or more unbelievable in this case). The number is 1:2.15 conversion.

It's a good book. It's a good cover. The description is pretty darn good too. It is NOT that good.

Converting at nearly 50% is not what's going on.

There will come a point in a few days or a week where the ads will look like they're getting impressions and clicks but suddenly the sales have stopped. Did my book suddenly become unpopular?

No, the ads stopped running and the reporting is just catching up.

Please read this last part again. You'll want to firmly cement this idea in your head because it can help you make decisions to run more ads faster.

If the ads truly stopped working on April 1, as a cruel April Fool's Day joke, then I would expect to see another 80 – 160 more clicks and impressions come in over the next three days with zero sales or downloads. Since I understand this will eventually happen, it doesn't make me panic.

Also, we learned that making a decision based on the AMS ACoS number can be dangerous.

Let's take the analysis one step further to show how dangerously wrong decisions can be to your bottom line.

Okay, right now I've spent $13.48 but remember I think there have actually been another 160 clicks that have happened but have not shown up on my report. Let's assume the actual spend is say 240 clicks times .17 per click or $40.80.

We're ignoring the KU page read revenue which will

mean our final profit result will be understated. We know we have 23 sales at $3.45 revenue each so that comes to $79.35.

Now, to calculate our estimated ROI with the added clicks we think are out there but haven't shown up yet, we take the pile of money we've made, which is $79.35, and subtract our estimated actual spend of $40.80 and get $38.55.

Next, we take the number $38.55 and divide it by the pile of money we estimate that the ad has actually spent, $40.80. This leaves us an ROI of 94.48%. And don't forget this is assuming ZERO KU page reads. I know from experience that the ROI is likely closer to 160% when I factor that in.

I want you to take a moment and consider a 94% ROI and what that means if one has scaled their ads to spend a lot more money. Imagine spending $100 per day at 94% ROI.

Your results would be revenue of $194 per day. That means $94 in profit every day. If you spend an hour per day on ads and do that every day, you're looking at $34,675 per year.

So that is a good number.

Actually, it's a great number. And I didn't even factor in read through to book 2 in the series which is excellent!

If you made a decision based upon ACoS to turn off your ads after day four because they were showing zero sales you'd be making a spectacularly bad decision.

We are not done with this example though. Let's do the same math with a different cost per click and see what impact the slow reporting has on your decision making.

Let's imagine that you ran that ad but the bid was .75 per click and the actual cost per click was .50. Let's also assume you've not read this chapter yet but were smart enough to understand the ACoS number wasn't worth trusting.

You take your actual clicks that were 82 times .50 and you've spent $41.00 but you estimate your revenue you estimate to be $79.35. Now, you don't bother to do any more calculations because you'll spend $41.00 to make $79.35 all day long.

But then I come along. You may call me the Grinch that stole ROI. I point out that the conversion rate seems a little too optimistic. I suggest you recalculate with 240. You shrug because nobody likes to be told what to do by the data Grinch. That's $120.00 but you shrug it off because you don't believe me.

A week later you notice that you're still spending a ton of money and the sales have slowed down to almost nothing.

What has happened?

You bid too much and now the reporting is catching up and snatching away all that profit you thought you had. The best decision when you did your original analysis was to turn off the ad. Nobody would make that call when it seems like they're making money.

This is why you need to analyze your data and understand what is truly going on.

In both of the last two examples I'd guess that 95% of people would make the wrong decisions. You can't have success running a business if you always make poor choices.

A person who makes this mistake with every ad will over time, probably when sixty days have passed and they spent a couple of thousand dollars on ads and only got back half what they spent, give up and declare to the world ads don't work.

Don't be that person. Please.

Does this mean that everyone who bids high is wrong?

No, not at all. Some of them may be losing money on the book with the ad but consider it a loss leader for the rest of their series. Or maybe they've just got a better book than you or I? Perhaps they have better ad copy?

We can learn from all sorts of sources.

I'm just asking that you the reader analyze your data and test everything to make the best decision for your business.

Do you now understand better the nature of how ads run? They go for a while and then stop. The numbers come in with a delay (which is clearly stated on the Amazon site) and we need to check their totals on ACoS with our own KDP data to decide if it is reasonable.

Let's take this analysis even further.

I have an ad that has a bid of .17 that is clearly profitable. After years of not bidding over .08 it can be tough for me to believe but I trust the data.

Knowing this what is my next step?

Spending an average of $2.28 per day isn't going to make me offensively rich. The next step is to consider what I can do to spend more.

As I've suggested there are three types of ads, Product Display – Interest, Product Display – Product, and Sponsored Product – Keyword.

I know that 99% of you focus on the keyword ads and ignore the other two. That's fine and it's exactly what I've been doing in a sense. I've focused only on the Product Display – Interest ads and ignored the other two.

These three types behave independently and show the ads in different spots. That means there are two other areas where I can run ads, hopefully get some clicks, and thus increase my daily spend and the wonderful revenue that goes along with it.

I need a plan.

Step 1: Run 5 more Product Display – Interest ads.

Product Display – Interest (PD - I) ads have no problem running at the same time as other PD – I ads for the same book.

Also, this only takes a few minutes to get into the system. I'm going to quite literally stop writing to go run them. I'll time it.

It took 13 minutes and 48 seconds.

The interests I picked were the same across all five. The budget was $1,200. The bid was as follows: two ads at .15, two ads at .17, and one ad at .20.

In 2 – 5 weeks some of those ads may start getting impressions, clicks, and spend. It is possible all the ads will get impressions. It is also possible that the ad that gets the most impressions, clicks, and spend won't be the obvious .20 bid ad. I've seen this more often than not. It's why I test.

The .17 ad worked great, but what if I could shave two cents off the bid?

What if the .20 delivers 500% more clicks, then the reduced ROI percentage won't matter as much as the substantial increase in total revenue.

These are the questions I think about when I'm making my plans.

Step 2: Run one Sponsored Product – Keyword ad.

I have a list of keywords that I use for this, but I don't remember how long it took to create. So, in the interest of data for you, the reader, I'm going to build a keyword list from scratch using KDP Rocket...while watching Game of Thrones and then eventually, if I move at slow pace, the semi-finals of the NCAA men's basketball tournament.

Building keyword ads is a bit tedious. (KDP Rocket's New KEYWORD Feature didn't exist when I wrote this section.)

There will also be snacking.

Okay, it took quite a while but I enjoyed some binge watching and basketball along the way.

Step 3: Run one Product Display – Interest ad.

This was my strategy to help scale one of my books and it's what I did just today. Don't be fooled into thinking I'm done writing ads for a while. I'm not. Tomorrow I'll probably run five more Product Display – Interest ads.

I'll keep an eye on the other two ads.

Scaling takes a lot of time, and one must look closely at their ads and continually be creating more of them.

# Chapter Twelve: Analysis Lesson 1

## Lesson One: Single Ad Analysis

Throughout the book, I'll be periodically giving you chapters where I analyze specific ads. It's my hope that these examples will help you start to learn which questions to ask yourself to determine how your ads are performing.

The art of analysis is, in short, about asking questions. We are going to look at an ad I ran for *Underwood, Scotch, and Wry*, which sells for $4.99. It was a Product Display – Interest ad, the bid was ten cents, the budget was $1200.00. It was named USW044 (1) (1). At the time, I had a different naming convention. This tells me that it was the 44th ad for this book, and it was the third time I'd copied it. The original ad was simply USW044.

The ad began its life on March 24, 2017. It didn't do

anything until April 1, when it had 16 impressions. The next day it had its first click on 220 impressions. The analysis I did for this ad happened on April 29.

How is the ad performing?

That's my first question. Let's analyze it the way most people do by looking at the ACoS number for this ad.

As of the April 11, my total spend was $13.60. The ads "Est. Total Sales" was $9.98.

So, according to the AMS report, I've only made $6.98 (70% of $9.98), which is actually closer to $6.92 when one factors in the delivery cost. Let's do some math.

$6.92 - $13.60= -6.68

Or calculating the ROI-$6.68/$13.60 = -49.11%

It seems this ad has cost me a little more than one Venti Chai Latte from Starbucks. That's bad.

But is it?

That's not how I analyze my ads, not even close.

> IMPORTANT: I believe that over the long run a click is a click is a click. Assuming one doesn't

do something insane like advertise their gothic horror sex romp novel with extra stabbiness to the cozy mystery crowd, then with few exceptions the clicks will all be equal once the person gets to your description.

I look at the data on the AMS report and keep several things in mind.

1. The reporting may be delayed.
2. The reporting does NOT include page reads.
3. The reporting may not be accurate with regards to sales results.

The first two are clearly stated on the AMS site. The third one is based upon my own experience. It's not important that I lay out a convincing argument as to why I believe that not all sales are captured, it is sufficient to say that this is what I believe and it informs my analysis.

Let's ask that question again. How is the ad doing?

I spent $13.60 and received 136 clicks at ten cents each. That's excellent. Normally, I'd stop there but that doesn't really help you the reader.

One of the metrics I watch pretty closely in my own data is the conversion rate for a description. As you know from Chapter Three, better ad copy results in better conversions. I know that *Underwood, Scotch, and Wry* consistently over the long run converts at 1:10. In other words one in every ten people who click on an ad will either buy the book or download it and read all the way through (Clicks/Sales + (page reads/KENPC).

Continuing on with the analysis that looks more like 13 sales or downloads.

I don't even need to do the math to know that this ad is running in the black, but again, that doesn't help you to learn.

> IMPORTANT: I'm able to do the following deeper analysis because I make sure to save my AMS data daily. From those reports, I'm able to subtract one from another and get the daily spend, impressions, and clicks by ad. I do this in Excel.

How do I get a better estimation of the real value of the ad?

Again, I believe that all clicks are created equal. If this is the case and I'm running other ads for this book, then one method of analysis is to assign the revenue from the sales and page reads during the time period studied (3/24 – 4/29) on a weighted basis.

The next thing I'll pull from my data is the total spend, impressions, clicks, sales revenue, and page read revenue. I don't actually use the impression or spend data, but I thought it would be nice to include it here.

*Underwood, Scotch, and Wry* totals from all ads from 3/24/17 – 4/29/17 follow:

1. Spend = $1,074.05
2. Impressions = 1,217,864
3. Clicks = 6,711
4. Sales Revenue = $960.90
5. Page Read Revenue = $376.11

It is clear that this ad, at this point in its life wasn't spending much compared to all the other ads running. $13.60 out of $1074.05 is only 1.26% of the total spend. But, this ad was getting me clicks at an average of 10 cents per click while the total group was averaging 16 cents per click.

Another point in this ads favor.

Now, let's calculated the weighted revenue from the ad.

I use the clicks to determine the weight.

136 clicks from the ad in question/6711 total clicks for all ads = 2.027%

My belief is that 2.03% of the revenue generated during that time period can reasonable be credited to the ad we're analyzing.

$1337.01 x .02027 = $27.09

Let's do the Starbucks Venti Chai Latte conversion again.

$27.09 - $13.60 = $13.49

That's at least a couple Venti Chai Latte result, which is good.

ROI = $13.49/$13.60

ROI = 99%

Summary: I believe the ad has yielded a substantial profit and I'll keep it running.

That's really all we're trying to do. We are trying to solve that age-old riddle posed by a group of English philosophers who went by the name The Clash, "Should I stay or should I go", which if one is familiar with the subtleties of British English means, "Should this ad keep running or should I send it to the digital rubbish bin?"

Do you see the difference in the results? Losing 49

percent ROI is different than making 99 percent ROI.

But why should you believe a middle-aged guy who may or may not be listening to Rock the Casbah as he types this?

That's a great question.

Arguments that the previous chapter is a load of bollocks. (Yes, I'm typing with a British accent and I feel cool because of it.)

> You're an idiot because you included all the sales for US&W but you have no idea if they all came from ads. Maybe some of the sales were organic? Maybe some of them were word of mouth?

Yes, that's a fair point. Let's look at both concerns.

Organic sales because of improved ranking from sales/KU downloads that were a result of the ads:

During the period in question the book was ranked at a low point of #14,326 on March 25, and was at #5700 on April 29th, with most of the days being #2646 and #5742. That means it was in the top 60 for one category and top 20 for another for most of that time. It is certainly within the realm of possibilities that a sale or two crept in organically.

Also, and this is something that doesn't get talked about. Amazon does re-targeting through Facebook. If you go and randomly click on an ad for a book there is a better than average chance you'll see an ad for it on Facebook in the near future. What if one of those re-targeting efforts actually led to the sale?

And what if a person who found your book organically told their friend who also bought it? That would really skew your results.

I don't care.

If I weren't advertising my book would probably be hovering around #150,000, there wouldn't be any organic sales, there would be zero re-targeting and because nobody is reading it, zero word of mouth.

In data analysis, we don't get hung up on micro details; we look at the macro picture.

Remember, all I'm trying to do is decide between letting it run or not. Maybe I'm trying to figure out if I should run more like it. Regardless, I don't need to know if it was truly profitable by 99% or 93% or even 72%. The point is that it was profitable, the click cost was great, and it was definitely not losing me money like the AMS report seemed to be indicating.

What does this mean for you the reader?

A couple of things spring to mind. One is that it will be much easier for you to do this sort of analysis if you start practicing with your first few ads. If you already have good sales or use other advertising venues, too, then it may be worthwhile to figure out a baseline for your revenue before the ads begin and then subtract that from your total revenue number.

For instance, if your book earns $10.00 a day and has been doing that for a month without any ads, go ahead and reduce the total revenue number accordingly. You'll have a more accurate estimate.

Secondly, after doing this a few times it will become easy to get a sense for how an ad is doing without actually needing to "do the math." That skill comes with practice but it will save you time.

The third thing you should remember is that if you're going to make all your decisions based upon only the AMS data, then you're completely screwed. You'll make all sorts of wrong decisions. You'll turn ads off that are actually crushing it and your children will likely stop loving you because the quality of their birthday gifts will decline substantially because of your horrible ad management and resulting loss in birthday present buying revenue. It's really up to you.

So ends the first analysis lesson. I hope you survived the maths (again, typing like a Brit).

# Chapter Thirteen: A Conversation about Descriptions

## A Conversation about Descriptions

This is a subject I'm passionate about because it can make the difference between a profitable ad and one that is just draining your bank account. Chapter 3 was all about descriptions and copywriting. Now that we've come a ways in the process, it is worth reminding you of the importance of a good description. I had the following conversation I had with a writer friend of mine on the subject and I thought it was good enough to include in the book.

Andrew Mackay is a British writer of satires. He's funny as are his books. We had a discussion about advertising and ad copy. I didn't want to hurt his feelings but since he had reached out to me for insight, I decided to mention that I thought his description copy could use a slight tweak.

Since he was British, I assumed that he knew that when one says a slight tweak, it meant massive change. He did. We got to work.

The description began:

In Their Shoes - The Teacher (British Comedy / Satire / Fiction) (Book 1).

He thought it was pretty good. He was mistaken. That opening line isn't a hook, I explained. I sent him to my satire and wrote, "Right after my hook, I go for some humor...Arthur Byrne is a lot of things...bitter, ambivalent, angst ridden, snarky, and more than anything...he's a writer who can't write anymore. So, naturally, now he's a professor."

I suggested he use some humor, I mean, that's his stock in trade and it's what people are looking for in their satires.

To which Andrew replied, "I see." Which, is a long winded British answer for the more succinct "huh."

A moment later he wrote, "Cheating, Lying, Skipping class...and that's just the staff!"

I wrote back, "NOW THAT IS A HOOK!!!" Followed by a "Bravo!"

It was so much better than what he had before. It doesn't take a copywriting rocket scientist to know that the first one was simply a line of fact and was boring.

When I told him to use some humor he immediately switched gears and came up with a much better start to his description.

We then went on to discuss the length of his paragraphs in the description. They were fairly normal looking if one were reading a book. Descriptions are NOT books. This isn't creative writing it's advertising copy. We want short and punchy. Often a single line will do.

If you've ever noticed the email blast you get from sites you've signed up for, the good "newsletters" will have one sentence (two at the max) paragraphs. There will be lots of short sentences between those "longer" paragraphs.

The idea is to move the reader through the copy to get to the call-to-action. We discussed this and he got what I was talking about and off he went to begin work on his descriptions for all his books.

He said, before parting, "Right NOW is the happiest and

most fulfilled I've ever felt since embarking on this journey."

Frankly, I have no idea what that means in British. I suspect he's mildly pleased.

If you've already forgotten what is in Chapter 3, go back and re-read it. Even if that messes with your obsessive-compulsive tendencies, you need to do it now and then take a break. I really want you to succeed and descriptions are crucial.

# Chapter Fourteen: What's Your Conversion Rate?

What's your conversion rate on your description?

"Brian, I don't want to mess with all of this, just tell me how to make money on my ads."

I know, believe me, I do. And it can get annoying when I tell you "This is IMPORTANT" every other line, but it truly is important. Knowing your conversion rate for your description will give you a tool to make decisions.

"You're a tool."

Please stay with me.

I want to give an example of two different conversion

rates and why knowing yours is important.

1. Description A converts at 1:30 (read one in thirty)

2. Description B converts at 1:10

Let's say you're running Sponsored Product Ads and paying 15 cents per click. Furthermore, your book is priced at $4.99.

Before you panic, I'm not going to do a ton of math, just a little.

Description A will either get a sale or a KU download one time per thirty clicks. Every conversion will cost $4.50. If it is a sale you'll be earning approximately $3.45. Depending upon your page count, the KU download, assuming the reader reads all the way to the end, will likely be less.

Do you see the problem? The ad will always be a failure at that conversion rate because $4.50 is more than $3.45. You're losing money.

You've probably already done the math on 1:10, but here it is anyway. The Description B conversion will cost $1.50, which is less than $3.50 and likely less than what you make on KU page reads.

That wasn't so bad, was it?

"No, I suppose not."

Good. What are the main points you should take away from this discussion?

"I don't know," you the reader said with a sigh really wanting to go to recess.

Yes, you do.

"Try to have a good description."

That's on the right track. But there is a lot more here if you read between the lines.

1. If your book is priced less than $4.99, then it will be even harder to have a profitable ad.

2. If your CPC is higher than 15 cents, it will be harder to have a profitable ad.

Assignment One:

Go ahead and look at the ads you've run and do the same sort of comparison with your price point and both conversion rates. Use the CPC of your most expensive ad and take a look at the potential for profitability.

    A. Your CPC x 30

    B. Your CPC x 10

    C. Compare that to how much you make for both a sale or a complete read through (KENPC x .005)

Is that a furrowed brow I see?

"Maybe."

Don't get frustrated or give up.

Assignment Two:

This may take a couple of weeks to complete, but the information you learn from it will be incredibly valuable.

Calculate the rate of conversion for one of your books, preferably the first book in a series or a boxed set. You can certainly do this exercise for as many books as you like, but since your ads are likely for only the first book or the boxed sets, it is these books that are going to give the best results.

What you need:

1. Daily clicks from all ads for the book in question.

2. Daily sales from the book (from KDP report)

3. Daily page reads from the book (from KDP report)

4. KENPC for the book (Kindle Edition Normalized Page Count)

How to find Daily Clicks:

1. Download the AMS report for your ads. (the black down arrow next to the "Results per Page" drop down on the page with your Advertising Campaigns).

2. Save this file in a folder with the date you downloaded it.

3. Wait 24 hours and download another report.

4. For each ad that pertains to the book description we're trying to analyze by subtracting the older of the two reports from the new one. This will give you the clicks for that 24 hour period.

5. Write that number in a notebook with the date or keep it in an Excel file. Be sure to include the

name of the book. (Note: It is best to do this for the first book in a series as your first test.)

6. Repeat for two weeks minimum.

How to find Daily Sales & Page Reads (can be done at the end of the 14 days):

1. Go to your KDP Dashboard.

2. Click on "Reports" at the top.

3. Change the date range on Filters, the line just above the red units daily graph. Choose a range of the last fourteen days, if you're doing this after having gathered 14 days' worth of Daily Clicks.

4. Click on the orange "Update Report" button.

5. Scroll down to the bottom and click on the orange "Generate Report" button.

6. The information you need for sales is in the Royalty Report tab.

7. The information you need for page reads is in the Orders Report tab.

How to look up the KENPC for your book:

1. Go to your KDP Dashboard.

2. Click on "Bookshelf".

3. Find the book you want to look up and click on the "Promote and Advertise" button.

4. Scroll down a bit until you see a box with the heading "Earn Royalties from the KDP Select Global Fund." The last line in that box will read something like "Kindle Edition Normalized Page Count (KENPC) v2.0: 420"

5. 420 is the KENPC page count (in this example), and that's how many pages you'll get paid for if a person reads your entire book.

Figuring out the conversion rate:

Before you do the calculation, there are a couple of things I'd like to mention. The first is that in statistical analysis there is a thing called variance. It isn't important that you understand variance in great detail, just that you know it exists. If you find that your book converts at 1:25, that doesn't mean you won't occasionally get three clicks with two sales. Conversely, you may also get 50 clicks with zero sales or downloads.

The second point that is worth understanding is that we are making a couple assumptions that by their nature are giving us a result that is likely a bit more conservative than the actual conversion rate. Meaning, you may calculate that it is 1:25 but it may really be 1:23.

Let me explain. First of all, there are two opposing forces that will skew the numbers. One, organic sales can come at any time. They don't happen terribly often when you're a relative unknown, but they do occur sometimes. This means there may be one or two extra sales that were unrelated to your ads. That's okay.

Secondly, we are going to calculate a download equivalent based upon the page reads. We make the assumption that 100% of the people that download your book will read all the way to the end. That is not likely. Which means that we may calculate 10 downloads but it was actually 14 downloads where several people quit on your book…the bastards.

When looking at these two opposing forces it is likely that there will be a greater number of conversions missed in the page reads count than will be extra in the sales count. Thus, your conversion may be slightly better than the results indicate.

Keep in mind that this conversion number is a guidepost. We'll talk more about what your results mean at the end.

Calculating the Conversion Rate:

I will work through a hypothetical example for my book *Underwood, Scotch, and Wry*, which is priced at $4.99 and is a satire. The KENPC equals 281.

1. Using your Royalty Report add up all the paid sales over the 14 days. USW = 90 sales

2. Using the Orders Report add up all the page reads over the 14 days. USW = 31,226

3. Add up all the clicks over that period from your data that you kept. USW = 2572

4. Divide the page reads by the KENPC. 31,226/281 = 111.12, but we'll round down to 111 to make it easy.

5. Add the sales to the download equivalent. 90 + 111 = 201.

6. Divide the clicks by the result in step 5. 2572/201 = 12.79

Our answer is 1:12.79. That's not bad at all.

If you continue to gather data and measure over a longer

period of time, because the people that downloaded the book in say the last three days (or 21% of your sample days) have not had time to finish the book, so there are page reads to come. This also means the number is a bit more conservative than reality.

The same book, with 60 days' worth of data, where the last few days only represent 5% of your sample days, gives a result of 1:11.

Analyzing Your Results

1. If your result was greater than 1:30, your description is less appealing to readers than a pile of cat sick.

2. If your result was between 1:20 – 1:30, you probably have long paragraphs and use the description to try to tell the reader about the story instead of using proper copywriting to hook them into buying the book. You probably didn't include the reader in the description. Meaning, "You'll love this book because…". Also, did you have a call to action at the end? I didn't think so.

3. If your result was between 1:15 – 1:20, your description may have a pretty good hook but still needs work.

4. If your result was 1:10 – 1:15 you've got a solid description that will serve you well for a long time but could probably be a little better. As you improve at copywriting, you'll want to revisit it and see if you can make a few changes.

5. If your result was 1:6 – 1:10, your description is killing it and you should celebrate with something from either the bacon or the chocolate food groups.

6. If your result was less than 1:6, you may need to check your math, or you have such little data that you've gotten an unreasonable number. Keep tracking your numbers until you have at least 1,000 clicks to use for judging the conversions. Below 1:6 is rare and likely unsustainable over the long run unless your name starts with J.K. and involves wands.

# Chapter Fifteen: Analysis Lesson 2

## Lesson 2: Five Ad Analysis

In lesson two of analysis we're going to look at five ads. They are all for the book *Underwood, Scotch, and Wry*, my satire priced at $4.99.

    1. USW APR 2017 (A) PD Interest = .15 bid
    2. USW APR 2017 (B) PD Interest = .15 bid
    3. USW APR 2017 (C) PD Interest = .15 bid
    4. USW APR 2017 (D) PD Interest (1) = .17 bid
    5. USW APR 2017 (E) PD Interest = .20 bid

For the sake of ease, we will just refer to them by A – E.

This range of bidding is a bit higher than my norm. I typically bid in the .08 - .10 range, but I wanted to see if bidding considerably more would yield a lot more impressions than I get with most of my ads for this book.

They did not.

Let's look at how they did compare to the other 157 ads I've run on US&W.

Ranked by most impressions:

1. A = 39th
2. B = 42nd
3. C = 45th
4. E = 53rd
5. F = 93rd

Ranked by highest CPC:

1. A = 6th
2. B = 7th
3. C = 9th
4. D = 4th
5. E = 1st

It should be noted that of my 157 ads, when ranking by most expensive cost per click, one only needed to go down to 19th place before all of the rest of them were less than .08 per click. That's 138 ads averaging .08 per click or less.

Those .08 ads have yielded 22,630,890 impressions and

153,054 clicks on a spend of $10,123.33. So, my average cost per click for the eight cents and below ads is .066 per click.

It is worth mentioning that of the 157 ads, 10 were Sponsored Product (Keyword) ads.

First Take Away: You don't need to overbid.

Let's look at how the five ads in this test performed against one another.

All of the ads except D started to generate reasonable impressions on day 8.

    1. A = 1710
    2. B = 1664
    3. C = 2063
    4. D = 3
    5. E = 1458

The .17 ad was dead last and the .20 ad was fourth.

What about Day 2?

    1. A = 4978
    2. B = 3873
    3. C = 4958
    4. D = 2

5. E = 2770

It wasn't until the ads had been running for 9 days that ad E had its first day where it won the impressions battle.

What about after 17 days of generating 1,000 impressions or more?

    1. A = 142,930
    2. B = 137,922
    3. C = 121,541
    4. D = 2,984
    5. E = 142,930

The most expensive ad finally made it into second place. Even so, was it worth paying a 33% premium on ad E? And what about ad D? It had a .02 higher bid than A – C and never got going at all.

Second Take Away: You don't need to overbid.

What we really want are clicks.

After 17 days of generating 1,000 impressions or more the clicks were as follows.

    1. A = 851
    2. B = 809
    3. C = 665

4. D = 20
5. E = 814

It is no surprise that ad E also ended up with the second most clicks. Of course, as I said, I had to pay five cents more for each of those clicks. A – C were getting me clicks just fine on their own.

Third Take Away: You don't need to overbid.

What about profitability?

The short answer is the 15-cent ads had a 20% ROI and the 20-cent ad had a -6% ROI.

Fourth Take Away: Stop over bidding!

What about the CTR (click through rate)?

1. A = .576%
2. B = .598%
3. C = .530%
4. D = .690%
5. E = .574%

Are you kidding me? The ad with the best copy and that led to the most clicks on a per impression basis was the hapless ad D. Seriously, it crushed the other four ads and yet that wonderful (by comparison) CTR didn't mean a thing when it came to the ad getting chosen to have impressions delivered to it.

Fifth Take Away: Don't worry too much about CTR.

I hope you'll look at this data and decide that it is valuable to run multiple Product Display – Interest ads on a single book at varying bid levels to do your own test.

Additionally, one should be aware that it is possible to have many PD – Interest ads for a single book running at the same time. In fact, there were two more 15-cent ads that I had started a few days before this test that had similar results as A – C throughout that entire time.

Read that last paragraph again.

When you get to the point that you want to scale your spend, multiple PD – I ads will help with that regard.

I also hope you'll notice how simple this analysis was to do. I just listed the ads and ranked them. I didn't do any fancy pants math. I just compared their impressions and clicks to each other. I did go a bit further to calculate the estimated ROI but it was pretty obvious without doing the math that the expensive ad was going to be a loser.

This should be a great moment for those of you who are a bit afraid of the analysis. Often times it is a simple as looking at the data and doing a sort in Excel.

Let's go back to the beginning and talk about what I was thinking when I ran the ads. "Hey, Brian, I wonder if we bid more for an ad if it will get a bunch more impressions?"

That was it. I started with a simple question and ran the test. Please try to make yourself ask question and then figure out what data you need to answer those questions. I needed a period of time with multiple ads at different price points all running simultaneously. The D ad let me down a little but it was still informative.

Assignment: Write down something that you believe to be true about ads and figure out how to prove or disprove it with a test. Then run the test.

This may be more of a challenge than you think. Just the act of thinking up the test will be helpful. You'll thank me later when you're presented with your Nobel Prize in Statistics.

Conclusion: We learned some valuable things in this test. But keep in mind it was one test, in one genre (satire), at one point in April of 2017. If I run this same test, albeit with lower bids, again, I may well get different results. I likely will get different results. This is another thing about thinking like an analyst; one never assumes that the answers one gets from a single test apply across the board, or that the results will hold true in the future.

You must constantly test.

# Chapter Sixteen: A Conversation with

# Jenny

A conversation with Jenny

Jenny: How long does it take to get impressions when you start an ad? I bid 11 cents, twelve hours later, nothing, so I bid 25 cents, 12 hours later nothing, 8 hours ago I bid 40 cents and still nothing! This is for Sponsored Ads and also Product Display ads.

Brian: Okay, stop right now. You're panicking.

First of all, unless your book is priced at $8.99 (like it is a boxed set), you may get crushed at 40 cents per click.

Some ads take a few days to start getting impressions. Often Product Display ads take 2 - 6 weeks to start.

Put the ad back to 11 cents.

Run a few new Product Display ads every few days.

Then be patient.

This takes a lot of work. It takes a long time. And it is totally worth it.

Also, try not to edit your ads and change the bids. That messes up your data.

Furthermore, the reporting is usually slow. This means you may have already gotten impressions and clicks at 11 cents, but because the report may not show them for a few days, you've messed up a really good ad.

Patience is the key.

Jenny: Thanks, Brian Meeks. You're right, I am panicking because it's a new release and I wanted to pump the algorithms by getting extra sales/page reads right away before the surge around day 5. I only got 5 sales today, on the third day of its release.

I did AMS ads late last year and was getting some clicks for 6 cents but that was a different genre, and I didn't make a profit. My book is 99 cents with a KENPC of

265.

Brian: Jenny, the motto of this group is "Don't Panic" and this applies to new releases, too.

I've done pretty well as an author and I don't ever do ANYTHING for my releases. Heck, when I released the third book in my science fiction series I never even told my list. I still haven't bothered.

The point is that ads, if done correctly, are all the juice one needs to get their book to sell well.

(Note: I'm not suggesting anyone follow my lead and have really stupid secret launches. I'm just saying I've succeeded in spite of myself.)

The things I would worry about are my descriptions. It's important to read Chapter 4: Conversions and Chapter 12: A Conversation about Conversions.

It will give some insight into how to write an effective description. Almost nobody has one that is optimized.

Tonight, I'm going to write a chapter about pricing. $2.99 isn't very much. I don't think the book buying public sees nearly as much difference between a book at $2.99 and $4.99 as Indie authors think they do. Nobody cares about the extra two bucks, especially when they're willing to pay five bucks for a cup of water run over coffee beans from Starbucks.

Having a big launch is nice. It isn't as vastly important as you imagine.

If you write a good book. If you tell stories people want to read. If you take the time to nail the description. And lastly, if you have patience, you'll do fine.

That's why we're here, to help people get a handle on things.

Jenny: Thanks, I've been doing pretty well for the last 2.5 years with romance – not 6 figures but I've been happy with my sales and then they halved in December and halved again last month, which is why I'm trying a new genre. I didn't advertise in my other genre much – just concentrated on releasing every 2-3 months but now nobody is buying those books.

Brian: I think you'll find advertising will keep those books selling.

Jenny: I'm actually worried about putting the price up to $2.99. I get what you're saying about people buying take away coffee for $5.00 but whenever I put my price up from 99 cents to $2.99 in romance, my sales at least halved even on a new release.

Brian: Okay, so do the math on your sales halving. Which is better, 50 sales at $2.99 or 100 sales at .99?

Jenny: Yes, the $2.99 but it's more like 20 sales at 99 cents and then 9 sales at $2.99.

Brian: So, let's say you get 7 sales at $4.99

1. 7 x $3.50 = $24.50
2. 9 x $2.00 = $18.00

That's a 36% increase in revenue.

Now, let's think about your ads under the three scenarios.

A. 99 cents, you have almost no margin. Your ads will lose you money.

B. $2.99, you have more margin and you'll maybe make a little.

C. $4.99, you have a fine amount of margin and it won't be hard at all to run ads profitably.

If you can run ads profitably, then you can run LOTs of ads profitably and have a really good spend.

And if you're running lots of ads, getting lots of clicks,

and then getting lots of sales, your ranking will improve.

If your ranking improves you'll get some organic sales, too, which is a bonus.

Are you still afraid to raise your prices?

Jenny: No, not to 2.99 because I need 2.99 readers not 99c bargain hunter/freebie seekers. Writing longer 2.99 books was the only way I started making decent money in romance, after writing shorter 99c books

Brian: Good. How long are the $2.99 books?

Jenny: It annoys me that people won't pay $2.99 for a decent book.

Jenny: My new release is 50K.

Brian: Sure, they will. They'll also pay $4.99. At 50K, you should be at $4.99.

Jenny: I'm not sure they will pay that much when it's only my second book in this genre and pen name. The first book was shorter and 99 cents.

Brian: Yes, they will, because you're going to run ads.

The person that clicks on the ads won't care who you are,

or how many books you have, they'll only care about "Does the description hook me enough to make this my next read?"

I included this conversation because it is similar to many that I have with authors who are just starting out. It is easy to jump to a conclusion because it's the way you buy books. Or maybe your gut is telling you that something won't work. Perhaps, the little voice in your head has been looking for reasons to tear you down?

The point is that one should always test their assumptions. That's what I do. As you improve at analysis, though, you'll find that your ability to have a hypothesis and be right will go up substantially. This comes with experience. It is another reason why taking the time to really understand what's going on in this book will give you a lifelong skill that will make every aspect of book marketing easier.

Experience is an excellent teacher, who may or may not be a hottie. You should totally have a crush on Mr. or Ms. Experience and follow them around like a puppy dog.

# Chapter Seventeen: Pricing

## Pricing Your Book

This is a subject you may not have spent much time thinking about. Most people tend to error on the side of underpricing when they start out. That's normal.

There is a fantastic rush when we get a sale. That endorphin hit of external validation is addictive. It's so addictive there are endorphin pushers everywhere we look. Facebook is all about micro hits of our new favorite drug. We post a witty comment and somebody likes it. Boom, we just got a hit.

It's the same with our sales. I still get excited when I see sales and I've had over 40,000 of them. You'd think I'd be over it by now, but I'm not.

It may seem like I'm going off on another one of my

trademark digressions, but I'm not. This is important to understand.

If you've had even one sale you know that feeling. "I can't believe something I wrote is being read by a person who didn't give birth to me!"

This leads to fear of changing prices. You don't want to mess with that rush and risk the post-sale high.

There is a second reason this chapter may make you uncomfortable. All of the marketing you've done before Amazon ads has likely been through the many venues that advertise FREE promotions and 99 cent deals.

The bump you've gotten from those promotions and the subsequent decline of sales afterward may have given you the impression that people won't pay more than just a dollar or three for your writing, or your genre's writing.

This is not true.

You may feel like any change you make could severely impact sales.

I'm going to explain why that fear isn't worth giving into at all. There are many things in life to be afraid of: running out of bacon, sleeping through a final exam, or answering honestly when your significant other asks, "Do these pants make my butt look big?"

Those are all legitimate fears. Let's look at why "sales dropping because of a price change isn't one of them."

Let's say you're getting five sales per day of your book at 99 cents. Your goal is to make five figures a month so you can have the confidence to find a significant other who will lie to you about your pants.

It has been shown that we humans are risk averse. We would rather avoid a risk that could lead to a small loss than take on a risk that has a high chance of leading to a large gain. It's in our nature. The key is to frame a risk vs. reward situation so that the little frightened voice in our heads will shut up.

Back to our example. You're making $1.85 from the five sales every single day. And it feels really good. These are your potential first 1,000 readers. At your current pace, you'll have sold 1,000 books in 200 days.

Now, what about that goal of five figures. Making $10,000 in a month would also feel good, you imagine. I can tell you it does.

The current state of thing is that the downside risk is $55.50 per month. The upside is making a pile of money, buying a new car, joining a gym, feeling good about how you look, going on a date, meeting someone special and living happily ever after.

"But Brian, I have a husband I adore, two wonderful kids, Lisa and little Jimmy, and a house in the suburbs."

I hear you. Your situation is dire bordering on unbearable. There is hope. And the answer lies in the price point for your book.

First of all, the length of the book does matter but you may be surprised to hear that it matters less than you think. I recently read a comment by a woman who priced her book at $3.99 because it was only 80,000 words. She has a perception of value that is out of line with what the buying public will pay for that many words.

I price my books that are between 50 – 60K at $4.99. The ones over 70K are $5.99. I'm likely going to shift all the prices upward later this year.

What if you have all novellas? What do you do then? I would bundle them and advertise the boxed sets. And please, if you've got three novellas at 20K each, don't be afraid to price it at $4.99 or above.

Secondly, you're still worried about seeing your sales drop. I get it. But think about it this way, if you have a higher price, you'll make more money. If you make more money, you'll be able to advertise more. When you get to the point that you're spending $2,500 per month you'll likely have north of 800 paid sales and another 500,000 plus page reads that month and total revenue in the $6,000 range.

So, 150 sales and making $55.50 per month or 800-plus sales and a boatload of page reads and $3,000 plus per month?

The bottom line is you will get more sales if you advertise with Amazon ads. If you want to do it profitably you'll need to have a larger margin. You'll also have to get over your fears.

Remember, nothing is permanent. If you truly want to crush it as a professional author you'll need to price your books like someone who is serious about this business.

Fictional Objections from Readers:

I'd like to take a moment to answer some of the questions and concerns the voice inside my head imagines you the reader might have about raising your prices.

Bob is a plumbing enthusiast who writes what he calls a Blue-Collar Thriller series centering on a tough guy, Robert "The Pipe" McSoggyPants. Bob asked, "I am more concerned with getting a good ranking than profit at this point. The low 99 cent price is to get more sales and a better rank. I don't want to give that up."

Bob, though you're imaginary, that's no reason to avoid writing your question as a question. Still, I understand your concern.

Let me tell you about my best ranking for *Underwood, Scotch, and Wry*, ranking wise. It was from September 11, 2016 when the book hit a rank of #988. On September 22, it dropped to #1006. Four of the days were ranked between #520 and #610. The book launched August 19, 2014, so more than two years earlier. That was 11 days in the top 1000 and it happened well after my launch.

Did I do that with a 99-cent price point? Nope. It was all at $4.99 and with Amazon ads.

My point is that you can have both good ranking and profit.

Susan a 79-year-old mother of three and grandmother of six, who enjoys knitting, kittens, and underground bare knuckle brawling, writes romance and asks, "Everyone I know prices their romance novels between 99 cents and $2.99. Don't I want to price at the same level so my books don't look overpriced?"

That's a great question, Susan. And the answer is no.

I want you to consider the entire market. Today, just searching on the Top 100 contemporary romance titles, two of the top 4 were priced at $4.99. Yes, many of the top ones were at 99 cents, but I'd wager that most of those were priced that way because they were running a special. If they had a BookBub promotion, then their time in the top 100 may be a temporary thing.

Still, one might argue that if you have a lot of books in the series with good read through, then you'll make your money on the other books. I can't argue with that logic.

Still, until you try out $4.99 and run a keyword ad and 20 Product Display – Interest ads, you won't know how your book will perform at that price level.

We want to figure out how to maximize profit both now and in the future. So, I'd still give it a try.

Katarina, a 38-year-old former model turned writer who hates children, asks, "This may not be pertinent, but I find life is a little lonely being single. It's just one hot yoga class after another squeezed between rounds of golf. Are you single?"

Katarina, that's an excellent question. Yes.

# Chapter Eighteen: What if I'm wrong?

What if I'm wrong?

That's a question I should have probably addressed before this chapter, but we're here now.

Everything in this book should be read, considered, and then looked at through the prism of your situation. You have experience with your books that gives you a level of knowledge I don't have and it should be factored into the equation.

All I want you to do is question everything, even me.

In the last chapter, we talked about pricing. My opinions in that chapter are based upon my own experiences and though I didn't go deep into my own data, my opinions are perfectly valid...for me. The ideas are worth considering. I'd do some tests.

Shawn Inmon, after reading the chapter, wrote, "Brian, I've come around to this way of thinking. For the last 18 months or so, I've kept my full price books at $2.99. About three months ago, I pushed most of them to $3.99, with no discernible drop off in sales. However, I left my newest release, which has been bouncing between 5,000 – 10,000 in the store, at $2.99. Three days ago, I moved it to $4.99. You want to know what's happened since? Nothing. It's selling just like it was before, except I'm making more money on each copy sold. And I'm okay with that."

Jenny Jones also read the chapter and followed my advice. She wrote, "I increased the price of my new release last night from 99 cents to $2.99. Yesterday, I had 26 sales at 99 cents and today I had 7 sales at $2.99, so I only made $5.00 more. I feel so sad.

Jenny had an increase of 61% in revenue but she was still upset because her ranking went down from the 5,000 range to the 12,000 range. She was worried about 19 potential newsletter subscribers. She believes that more sales with less revenue is better for her situation.

That's okay. Everyone has different goals.

There are other factors that would go into a person's decisions.

1. How many books are in the series?
2. What is the read through?
3. What is the series value of a sale of book one?

This last point probably needs a little explanation. Warning: There will be math.

Imagine you have four books in your series.

Before we talk about the price of book one, let's consider books 2 – 4. Let's say that they are all $4.99. That means that each one yields approximately $3.45.

If a person reads book one and loves it enough to read the remaining books that will add an additional 3 x $3.45 or $10.35.
Not all people love book one and won't read any further.

So, we have those that will read book one through four and those that will only read book one. Also, there will be some that read only part way through the series and lose interest.

Here's the question, what is the value of the series when a person buys book one?

This is how you calculate the answer to that question for your series. It is more accurate with books that have been out a while. Also, if the first three books were out for a while and then there was a gap between book four, then naturally it may not have as many sales as you would truly expect for the read through.

For this example, I'll use my *Henry Wood Detective* series in which the fourth book has been out since July 2014. That means we have lots of data. It should be noted that my read through on this series is NOT great. Don't assume your numbers will be as bad as mine.

1. What is the historical read through from book 1 to book 2?

2. Lifetime sales of book one = 8,995

3. Lifetime sales of book two = 3,740

4. Divide book two by book one (3,740/8,995 = .416)

Okay, so we know that just over 41% of the people who read my 1955 noir mystery series with a time travel closet will want to read book 2. (Yes, I said time travel closet. It's a long story.)

Go ahead and do that rather easy math for your series.

The next step may be a little different than you expect so read the steps closely.

1. What is the historical read through from book one all the way to book three?

2. Lifetime sales of book one = 8,995

3. Lifetime sales of book three = 2,648

4. Divide book three by book one (2,648/8,995 = .294)

We will need to do this for each book in the series. If you have six books, then you'll just keep moving down the line but always remember to divide the total for each book by book one. That's the number we need to do our final calculation.

1. What is the historical read through from Book 1 all the way to Book 4?

2. Lifetime sales of book one = 8,995

3. Lifetime sales of book four = 1,827

4. Divide book four by book one (1,827/8,995 = .203)

The last set of steps will give us the total series value for a reader who comes in at book one.

1. Revenue from book one x 1.0 (or 100%). $3.45 x 1 = $3.45

2. Revenue from book two x .416 (or 41.6%). $2.75 x .416 = $1.14

3. Revenue from book three x .294 (or 29.4%). $4.15 x .294 = $1.22

4. Revenue from book four x .203 (or 20.3%). $4.15 x .203 = $0.84

What is the total of all of those numbers added up? It's $6.67

What is the total if I price book 1 at .99? It's $3.57.

I've had my first book in the series at 99 cents for short periods of time. When I raised the price from $2.99 to $3.99 I couldn't detect any drop off in sales. When I went from $3.99 to $4.99 it was the same thing. The sales stayed consistent as measured by my conversion rate for the book. People didn't seem to care.

But let's apply what happened to Jenny's numbers, admittedly only one day, but still interesting and see what that would mean if she had four books in her series with the same read through and price as mine.

1. $3.57 x 26 readers that bought book one at 99 cents = $92.82

2. $6.67 x 7 readers that bought book one full-price = $46.69

It is clear that if she had a four-book series and they were priced the same as my books in the example with the same read through, then her 99-cent price point is the way to go.

The point is you need to test. I've tested 99 cents and permafree on this book. I have the data to support my pricing decisions. I encourage you to "do the math" on your books.

I can't stress this enough. Test these theories with your books. Genres vary and you need your own data.

Cherise Kelley, who writes romance, wrote, "I priced my 50k (words) romances at $2.99. I upped on to $3.99

briefly and revenue fell."

Wendy Farley Wang wrote, "I just raised the prices on my best-selling series (2 books) to $3.99 last week with NO change in sales and an increase in reads. I had already upped my price on my older series to $3.99 for all the books over 50k (words). These books are each between 60k – 90k. Taking all my books over 50k to $4.99 scares the bejeezus out of me. I may have to work up to it."

Adam Croft, who writes crime fiction and psychological thrillers and has sold over 1 million books, wrote, "I completely agree in theory, Brian, and I'd love that to work for me. But my books sell in far greater numbers and make me more money when priced at £1.99/$2.99. If I lower the price, I sell more copies but make less money. If I raise the price even a dollar, copies sold and money earned both bomb. That for me is the 'sweet spot', despite constantly experimenting to try and get different price points to work (especially when running paid ads). Maybe it's something that's peculiar to my genre — I don't know. All I know is I'd love to raise my prices, but it never seems to pay off."

# Chapter Nineteen: Exclusive vs. Wide

Exclusive v s. Wide

This is a sensitive subject. Maybe not as much as politics, religion, or who's better Ohio State or michigan? (Just kidding, it's obviously the Buckeyes...and no, that's not an editing mistake...michigan is never capitalized.)

This is a look at the value of going exclusive with Amazon when an author is running AMS ads.

I started out just on Amazon when I began mostly because I hadn't figured out how put my books up on the other sites. Eventually, I got around to iBooks, Kobo, and Barnes & Noble.

My motivation was to try to get a BookBub ad. It worked.

I later went back to being exclusive when KU came out. It was okay. I went wide again and then finally two years ago went back to being exclusive.

There are many reasons to go wide. I have a friend who does much better on iBooks than on Amazon and he does well on Amazon.

Not everyone does great wide. I had one good wide month at $1000 worth of profits and the rest were usually below $100 in revenue.

There is one reason for wide that people often cite that I believe is misguided. And that's the "What if Amazon does… (Fill in some sort of post-apocalyptic scenario)?" It drives some authors to go wide out of fear.

That argument is a two-sided coin. The other side is "What if Amazon doesn't wake up one day and decide to do something terrible to the people who are making them a giant pile of money?"

Over the last two years, I'd estimate my revenue had I stayed wide at somewhere in the $20 – 40K range. That's less than the than $160K plus I've made, with 47% of that being from KU page reads.

For me being exclusive is the right answer.

Is it the right move for you?

I don't know, but it's easy for you to find out. Of course, this would be just an estimate, but let's do a little thought exercise.

Let's say you intend to really dedicate the time and energy to do Amazon ads. Since you bought this book I don't think that's a huge leap.

Now, let's look up how much you've made over the last six months being wide (not including the Amazon revenue). Write that number of a piece of paper.

Okay, go ahead and write down the amount of money you made from Amazon.

Keep in mind that nearly half of my revenue comes from page reads. With this in mind, go ahead and write the Amazon number down again. Yes, you've written it twice.

The first number we're going to imagine is your page reads if you had been exclusive. Is it bigger than the total of all the wide venues combined than there is a good chance you would have made more being exclusive and running AMS ads.

What's more, as you continue to improve at AMS marketing, and dig into the Product Display – Interest ads, which I hope by this point in the book you've realized are a viable part of your plan, you'll see your sales revenue grow and your KU page read number climb as well.

Any comprehensive AMS marketing plan that I would suggest will contain many more Product Display – Interest ads than keyword ads. The main benefit is that PD – I ads run on people's Kindles.

KU subscribers see these ads, and to them your book priced at $4.99 is free. Yes, you're getting the benefits of a perma free book without losing the benefits of having it on sale.

You get the ranking help when the KU person downloads your book and that benefit is on the paid rankings not the free rankings.
Being exclusive and running a ton of Product Display – Interest ads is a great option.

Again, I'm not looking to start a fight. Some people cherish their decision to be wide and if you suggest otherwise they take it as a personal affront. Please don't be upset by my suggestions. I'm only asking that you take a few minutes and do an analysis of your situation. Nobody will know you did it.

If the data shows you're doing better on the other

platforms than you would be on Amazon, then stay wide. If you want to stay wide because it makes you happy, then that's a good reason, too. If you're doing it out of fear, please reread the chapter.

If you do stay wide, it will make it more of a challenge to crush it using Amazon ads.

This is just my take on the value of being exclusive as it pertains to using AMS ads. It's up to you.

# Chapter Twenty: The Most Asked Question

## The Most Asked Question

Why did my ads stop working?

Authors new to AMS marketing may not have thought about the life of an ad until their first good ad dies. It's easy to see the clicks coming in and to start imagining that you've unlocked the secret and those 100 clicks per day will always be there. A week later they're gone.

What happened?

The answer is the ad ran for a while and then it stopped getting impressions because that's how ads work.

Unfortunately, there isn't a great rule of thumb (or any of your digits) that will tell you how long each ad will run. Just like there isn't a way to know when an ad will actually begin to generate impressions.

It's frustrating. I know and that's just the way things go.

Do you remember the ad we looked at in Chapter 11? At the time I wrote that chapter, the ad had only delivered 136 clicks at ten cents each. It didn't deliver the first click until day 10. The click totals by day were 1, 2, 3, 2, 16, 15, 22, 17, 3, 1, 0, 0.

What I want you to see in that list is how there were a few clicks and then a peak over four days and then back down to only a few and eventually zero.

That's the sort of thing that might make a novice Amazon ads runner scratch their head.

What should one do when this happens?

Well, I'll tell you what I did. Nothing.

The ad continues on barely doing anything: 2, 2, 1, 2, 2, 0, 1, 0, 3, 6, 6, 8, 13, 2, 6, 2, 2, 1. Yes, another tiny increase over a six-day span and then back down to almost nothing.

The next day was a zero.

The day after that was nine clicks.

Then from nowhere a run of four days that was worth being happy about: 103, 79, 105, 77, and then back to 16, 9, 2, 7, 4, 0, 4, 0, 0, 0.

This is how I analyze that ad. It ran for four days. The four days north of 77 clicks are what I consider to be an ad that is running. One and two clicks aren't even worth worrying about. It should be noted that that run didn't happen until six weeks after the ad was approved.

Does that mean that we can only expect four good days from our ads?

Nope.

Do you remember those ads in Chapter 14? The three ads where I bid at 15 cents all delivered an average of 30 plus clicks per day from 4/9/2017 – 5/14/2017. That's over a month of consistent results. The only reason they stopped is because I paused them since my new 13-cent ads were starting to get impressions.

Why do you suppose some of the ads delivered more consistently than the others?

One might guess it was because of the bid, but then I'd say go back and look at the ad where I bid 17 cents and see how it did. It never got running.

I do think that higher bid ads will run longer. This is where you need to keep a close eye on your daily numbers and compare one ad to the next. You need to look for explanations. And most importantly, you need to continue to look for exceptions that might prove your theory wrong.

This last point is important.

If you believe that only .25 ads will work for your book, based upon two ads, well, you'll never do too well at Amazon ads. Not because you're bidding so much, though that's part of it, but because you'll miss out on all the clicks you could have at much less. You won't even run lower bid ads because you're sure that they will do nothing, so why test? You won't become a master. I've said this quite a few times in the book but it bears repeating. You need to constantly test.

Let's keep looking at ads.

The next one is not from one of my books but from an author friend's book, a thriller. It's a Sponsored Product – Keyword ad that started on 2/24/2017 and as of 5/3/2017 was still live, though for all intents and purposes it was dead. Don't cry for this ad, Argentina. It had a good life.

1,996,052 impressions, 2813 clicks, a spend of $263.29 for an average CPC of .083 or just over eight cents per click.

This is by any measure a superstar ad. It crushed it. The last few days of its life, while comfortably resting in a home for the aged ads, it had clicks of 16, 18, 18, 31, 139, 10, and then never made it over 10 again. The 139 clicks came on April 10, 2017. By early May, at the request of its family, the plug was pulled. Still, it had a good run.

It's worth repeating that this ad over its life had nearly 2 million impressions and delivered clicks at just over eight cents apiece.

While it is impossible to tell how long an ad will live a productive life, I have found that if I watch all my ads daily clicks, I'll start to see patterns. This is a skill that comes with time.

# Chapter Twenty-One: Create a Plan

# to Scale

## Scaling

This chapter has come toward the end because it requires understanding all of the aspects of Amazon ads we've already discussed.

If you've got a pretty good grasp of the previously discussed concepts, then you're ready to start scaling. Be warned, though, it is tough and not everything you do will work.

Authors will need to scale in their own way. Some of the things to consider when building your scaling plan follow:

1. Price point

2. Series read through

3. Exclusive or wide

4. Bundles/Box sets

Here are some questions that you should know the answer to, or if you don't, should figure out and write down.

1. What is the conversion rate for your descriptions by book? (Chapter 12)

2. What is the read through value of your series? (Chapter 16)

3. What is the range of days that an ad typically delivers greater than 10 clicks?

4. On average, how many days do your ads run (generate more than 10 clicks per day)?

5.
   Calculate for Keyword Ads
   Calculate for Product Display – Interest
   Calculate for Product Display – Product

6. On average how many days does it take for an ad to start delivering impressions and clicks?

Calculate for Keyword Ads
Calculate for Product Display Ads

Let's create a sample plan to increase your spend and scale up.

Answers for Henry Wood Detective series:

1. Converts at 1:12

2. Read through value $6.67

3. Range of click days 12 – 46 across all types of ads

4. Ad run time:

    10 Days- Keyword
    21 Days - Product Display - Interest
    15 Days - Product Display - Product Days

5. Start days:

    1 - 5 Days - Keyword
    8 Days - Product Display - Interest

IMPORTANT: The average number of days an ad will run varies greatly. These are my numbers as of the writing of this chapter. They are constantly changing. Keeping an eye on how long an ad is productive is one of the MOST IMPORTANT things to track.

ALSO IMPORTANT: While my most recent batch of Product Display – Interest ads got running at 8 days, this is NOT typical. Most of my historical data shows 2 – 6 weeks for these ads to start. Again, this is something you should keep an eye on because it can definitely change over time. Your planning depends upon knowing this number.

Figuring Out a Plan

The above mentioned answers to my questions are what I start with and from there I begin my thought process. I don't want to go all William Faulkner up in here on you but there will be a bit of stream of consciousness involved. I hope that if you can read what I'm thinking about, it will help you to get in the right head space to build your own plan.

Voice in my head: You've been letting your ads slide a bit since you started writing this book. You better step up your game or everyone that buys the book will be doing better than you. That would be embarrassing.

Brian: I need breakfast.

Voice: Grab your computer, go to the Market Café, order the eggs Benedict, and on the way think about your plan.

I grabbed my keys and hopped in the car. Working on ads is as much a mental exercise as it is actually writing the ads.

Brian: Okay, let's start with the *Henry Wood Detective* series. It has dreadful read through compared to the other books, but the people who do read the whole series often become readers of my other series. It seems that if they can get past the stupid time travel closet, they're up for my other shenanigans. Also, historically, the series ROI has been around 200%.

Voice: Good, so what do you need to buy clicks at to maintain that ROI? How about some driving math?

Brian: Well, if the series read through value (excluding readers who then finish and jump to other books of mine) is $6.67 and I want an ROI of 200%, then working backward, knowing I have a conversion of 1:12, I need to spend one third of $6.67 or $2.22 on each conversion.

Voice: Did you really just do all of that math in your head?

Brian: Yes, I had really good algebra teachers and math is

our friend.

Voice: Aren't you worried that if you put that in the book most readers will roll their eyes and give up?

Brian: I wasn't until now. Okay, let me explain. If the pile of money I'm going to make from a single conversion is $6.67 and I want to make 200% ROI, then the amount left over after I subtract the spend from the $6.67 needs to be twice as large as the spend. So, I just imagined two piles of money. One was twice as big as the other. But, now here is the kicker, the smaller bag plus the larger bag also equals $6.67. So that means that we have the equivalent of three smaller bags, or as I wrote, thirds. Then I just divided $6.67 by three which is (rounding down to account for whole cents) $2.22.

Voice: I'm sorry I asked.

Brian: Do you think the readers would like me to state it as an actual algebra problem?

Voice: No, I do not.

Brian: Fair enough, back to the question at hand, how much do I want to spend per click? Well, if I know that it will take 12 clicks to convert, on average, and I would prefer not to spend over $2.22, then that's almost $2.40, which is 20 cents per click, so if I set a goal of 18 cents per click, I should be just fine.

Voice: What does that mean for your ads?

Brian: I'll not bid over 36 cents on keyword ads or 18 cents on Product Display – Interest.

Voice: What about Product Display – Product ads?

Brian: I'm not quite sure on those yet. I need to give it some thought. Recently, I've been experimenting with random products unrelated to books. I've been bidding between 3 – 5 cents on these random ads and getting a few thousand impressions but only one click thus far. It hasn't proved conclusive but I might try some of those ads in addition to doing a more normal ad with book titles. The latter I'll likely bid at 18 cents, the former I may try at 10 cents.

Voice: You haven't talked about this in the book. What are these random ads?

Brian: Yes, but that's because I don't have any conclusive data. I have all sorts of ideas I test but I'm not going to pass along my theories if I can't say for sure they work. I hope that people will come up with their own crazy ideas.

Voice: Fair enough. Continue.

Brian: I need to order first.

Stomach: Please get the eggs Benedict...please, please, please!

Brian to waitress: "I'll have the eggs Benedict and a glass of water, please."

Stomach: Yay!

Voice: Don't even think about flirting with the waitress. She can do better than middle-aged and angst ridden. Get back to work.

Brian: That was hurtful, but you're right. Okay, so how many ads should I run and when?

Voice: That's the question and I wonder if you should consider building some more keywords for this series. Didn't you want to do some testing with gender-specific ad copy?

Brian: Yes, I did, though I thought I'd use the *Magellan Apocalypse* series for that test as I've not done any advertising for it in over a month so I've got a great baseline with which to compare the results.

Voice: And you don't think the gender specific ad copy will work on the mystery series?

Brian: It might work and the more I think about it, I might try a set of female-specific Product Display – Interest ads and target all the romance interests. I've recently learned some interesting data about romance readers and what other genres they like, and mystery was at the top of the list.

Voice: Romance is really competitive; won't it be more expensive?

Brian: Yes, I'll definitely need to bid 18 cents on those, but my theory is that by highlighting the strong female characters I may be able to have a better conversion rate.

Voice: Yes, but you're not changing your description to female-centric copy, are you?

Brian: No, but I might try changing my description for the *Magellan Apocalypse* boxed set to female-centric ad copy, since that is the one description that still needs to be reworked. It would take about an hour and then I could compare the female-centric ads for the first book in the series where the description is neutral to the ads for the boxed set. This could shed some further light on the impact that the original ad copy has on conversions. I currently believe it is minimal because I suspect most people forget the original ad copy by the time they start reading the description but I might be wrong.

Voice: Okay, so that's some good ideas for the science fiction series but let's get back to the plan for the mystery series.

Brian: I think I do want to try some copy highlighting Celine but she doesn't enter the series until book 2, though Lana and the other woman who has the butler named Winston...

Voice: Are you telling me you don't remember the name of your characters?

Brian: Yes and leave me alone. The point is there are two strong women in book one, even if the strongest woman in the series doesn't start until book two. So, I need to think of some copy that speaks to that fact and I'll use it to target romance readers.

Voice: What was Garrison Keeler's opening line about Lake Wobegon? It's funny and says something about how strong the women are and that might give you some ideas.

Brian: I'll Google it!

Voice: I can't wait.

Brian: "Lake Wobegon, where all the women are strong,

all the men are good looking, and all the children are above average."

Voice: Garrison Keillor is a much better writer than you.

Brian: Yes, he is! So, can we take his idea and build upon it? Henry's a clever detective who's fortunate he met Lana, the damsel in distress who just might save Henry right back.

Voice: If you use the word "damsel" won't you just piss off most women?

Brian: Maybe, let's try something else. A tough guy detective and two women who are as smart as they are good looking, but will it be enough to hold off Tommy "The Knife"?

Voice: That won't work for the headline. It's too long.

Brian: I should go check and see if it fits in the Product Display – Interest text section. If it does, I'll figure out another headline, since I really only care about the text in those ads since that is what shows up on the Kindles.

Voice: Did it fit?

Brian: Yes, with nineteen characters remaining. I went with "Smart women keep Henry on his toes." for the headline. I bid 18 cents and $1,200.00 budget. I didn't select any of the mystery categories, instead going for romance and literature. I named the ad HWDA June (A) PD_I F, indicating it was one of my female-centric ads. I need to write five more of these. I'll likely do bids of .18, .16, .16, .15, .15, .15, .15.

Voice: Okay, that's six ads for Book 1 in the Henry Wood Detective series. It's a good start.

Brian: I should also run those same six ads for the boxed set using the same bids, budget, and interest targeting. I'll likely do some ad copy that is focused on Celine though.

Also, I should run six ads for each book with my normal generic copy and mystery/thriller interests

Voice: That's 24 Product Display – Interest ads. What about keyword ads?

Brian: I'm thinking I'll do one ad for book 1 and one for the boxed set. I'll bid 36 cents with $100 per day budget.

Voice: Only two keyword ads?

Brian: Yes, for now, but we are just starting. On my list of things to do is build an even larger list of keywords using KDP Rocket. It's really time consuming so that will have to come after I get my base ads done for all three series and all three book one in the series.

Voice: What about Product Display – Product?

Brian: I need to increase the number of book titles for mystery but if I use the ones I have now, I should make a set of three different ads, at .18, .16, and .14 for both book one and the boxed set.

Voice: That's thirty ads for the mystery series.

Brian: I think a similar strategy for the science fiction series is a good idea, so that would take me to 60 ads. The satire series though, I'll keep doing what I've been doing and run another 15 Product Display – Interest ads at .15, .13, and .10, say five each. That's 75 ads.

Voice: How long will that take?

Brian: It will take all freaking day, but that's part of the deal. When those 75 are done, I'll need to figure out when I need to start adding more ads. Right now, it would seem that the PD-Interest ads will need to be revisited in a couple of weeks, just to be safe, 21 days at the latest. The keyword ads will be watched daily and since they start rather quickly, I'll not think about the next set until I've seen the clicks and impressions drop off their highs.

Also, after the full day of ads, today, if I really want to scale up, I can devote the time to increasing the keywords and products. Also, I might run another dozen or so of the random unrelated product ads I've been testing.

Voice: Well done, now pay your bill and get home, you've got more ads to write.

And that's a typical thought session for building my plan. I don't do them as often as I should. I would expect that if I get all those ads written today, I should be able to get back to spending around $4,000 per month, as I've let my own ads slide while I've been writing this book.

# Chapter Twenty-Two: Random Days

# of Awesome

## Random Days of Awesome

This chapter is simply a story of what might happen a couple of times per year. It's a glorious occurrence and may cause you to think your ship has come in, but it hasn't.

I've seen this happen a few times to me, and it usually lasts for one day or maybe a couple. I once had a week of such spectacular awesomeness that I was sure that little island off the coast of Grenada that's for sale would soon be mine. It's priced at $100 million.

Though these super days are rare, I still want you to be aware that they exist so that you will know the best course of action.

Bonnie Paulson is a delightful woman, happily married, six kids, and 40 chickens. She also has 39 books across several genres and a couple of pen names. As of the writing of this chapter she's mostly wide (all but 2 books).

As I've mentioned, being wide makes it more of a challenge to have a positive ROI because there isn't any of that bonus page read money. Bonnie is a great example of someone who's wide and can still do well at Amazon ads.

She's just started and still has a lot to learn. At this point, she's just following the advice learned from this book and doing her best. Today, I looked at her data.

This chapter is about her data for Monday, May 22, 2017. It was one of those days.

One of the metrics I look at to determine if an ad is truly running is whether it's delivering more than 1,000 impressions in a day.

I the days prior to her Manic Monday, she had 4, 2, 4, ads with 1,000 or more impressions. Her spend on those days were $1.91, $0.74, and $0.34. Her clicks were 15, 5, 4.

On Manic Monday, she had $53.89 in spend and 528 clicks.

Her sales jumped, her revenue jumped and the next day the spend and clicks went right back down.

The days following were $2.32, $2.93, and $3.03, which was better than the days before but not in the $60 per day range. Her clicks also stayed higher at 21, 28, and 27.

It should be noted that before Manic Monday she was getting clicks at around 12.4 cents per click. After the Manic Monday, she averaged 8.6 cents per click. Do I think there is any correlation? Probably not, but as of the writing of this chapter there isn't enough data to form a conclusion. What I want you to do is look for interesting things like a CPC drop, and then be aware of it as you study your data moving forward. Maybe there is a hidden gem of knowledge in there and maybe there isn't, but if you keep looking one day you'll find treasure.

The number of ads running with more than 1,000 impressions over that seven days was 4, 2, 4, 20, 6, 6, 6.

If you're new to Amazon ads you may tear your hair out trying to figure out what happened.

I don't do that. I'm balding.

The point is, I've looked at her data and there isn't anything to indicate anything special happened except that for one glorious day a bunch of existing ads fired up and crushed it. They were mostly keyword ads.

I hope this happens to you one day. I also hope you'll remember this chapter, celebrate how fun it was, and then realize that the next day is likely to be a disappointment. Don't let day 2 ruin your mood.

Just keep moving on with your ads and you'll be fine.

# Chapter Twenty-Three: Analysis

## Lesson 3

### Keyword Ad Short Run

One of the ideas I've been talking about is watching your data and looking for patterns. A pattern isn't something that needs to happen 100% of the time to be a valid clue. It may a large percentage of the time or it may only occasionally happen like in the last chapter.

If you recall, that chapter was about the occasional random day of awesome. The pattern I speak of is that these days happen and when they do, they are a one-day wonder. That's the pattern.

In keyword ads, there is a pattern that I notice happens a fair amount. I call it the short run.

Let's look at two ads by Bonnie Paulson.

They are from two different series but were started on the same day.

Here are the impressions for the first five days of each ad.

    1. First ad

Day One = 23,974
Day Two = 12,391
Day Three = 12,392
Day Four = 4,451
Day Five = 380

    2. Second ad

Day One = 22,958
Day Two = 12,841
Day Three = 13,013
Day Four = 4,692
Day Five = 304

These two are great examples of short run ads. Obviously, the daily impressions dropped considerably. But just so we're clear on the drop, as some people see numbers but don't truly SEE them. Here are the same numbers using the first day as the baseline and then the corresponding percentage change from Day 1

1. First ad

Day One = 23,974, which is 100% of day one, obviously.
Day Two = 12,391, dropped by 48.3%
Day Three = 12,392, dropped by 48.3%
Day Four = 4,451, dropped by 81.4% compared to day one
Day Five = 380, dropped by 98.4%

2. Second ad

Day One = 22,958, 100%
Day Two = 12,841, down 46.4%
Day Three = 13,013, down 45.7%
Day Four = 4,692, down, 80.4%
Day Five = 304, down 98.7%

You'll notice that in day three of the second ad, the impressions were slightly higher, which often happens in short runs. The main thing, though, is that by day 5 the ad is getting less than 2% of the impressions it was getting on Day 1.

Short runs can happen anytime. It isn't just from day one. An ad can be tooling along with less than 1,000 impressions per day, which as you recall, I don't consider to really be "on" and then shoot up to 50,000 impressions. More often than not, from that first day, there will be a short run like in Chapter 18.

In Chapter 19 there was a four-day short run for that ad that happened at the six-week mark. In that chapter I looked at the clicks and you can certainly do the same.

Let's look at another pattern.

This one is so common and has been discussed in such great detail in forms and such that I won't go into great detail.

You've got a keyword ad and you start another keyword ad with the same word for the same book. The moment the second keyword ad starts getting impressions the first one stops.

Does this happen all the time, as some believe?

No, it does not, but it happens frequently enough that you want to be aware of this pattern.

So, what do these two patterns mean to your strategy once you're aware of them?

That's a great question. I'm glad I asked it! (Just gave myself a high-five)

When I have a short run ad, especially with keyword ads, I immediately run another. Do I care if that ad causes the original ad to stop delivering any impressions? No, it's already dead.

You might be wondering if the ad will ever come back?

Well, that's another pattern you can look for, because I usually leave the ad on just for this reason. The answer is that they rarely come back.

If you want to increase your spend, keep an eye on ads that have died, whether from short run disease or just of natural causes, and then get a new ad into the game. If ten ads in a row die after four days and you're constantly putting up new ads, you'll have much more consistent results.

Many of the authors I've spoken with who are new to AMS ads wait far too long before giving up on one ad and trying another. Hopefully, you'll keep a close eye on your data and spot when it's time for another ad.

# Chapter Twenty-Four: Keyword List

# Building

Most people go through a shift in mindset during the early weeks of running Amazon ads.

It often begins with trepidation. How quickly will Amazon blow through my budget? This is especially true for people who've worked with Facebook ads. Facebook is happy to spend your money. In fact, they almost always spend your entire daily budget.

When a Facebook marketer comes to Amazon ads, it seems reasonable to have similar expectations. It doesn't take too many ads before they realize that the $5.00 per day budget isn't coming close to getting spent.

At first this doesn't matter because the ads haven't yielded any sales. Then, as if by magic a sale appears and the neophyte Amazon ads runner does the math. The ROI makes them giddy. It only takes a moment to go from giddy to what now?

They want to spend more money.

Just seeing an ad have a positive ROI starts one considering the possibilities if only they could increase the spend by two, three, twenty times. Visions of fame and fortune dance through their minds as they stare at the dashboard. But still the question persists, what now?

It is best to consider Product Display ads and Sponsored Product ads as two different market places. And even further, Product Display - Interest and - Product as their own markets, too. They behave differently, and if we ignore any of the three we're losing out on the opportunity to increase our spend.

Before we layout a plan, let's talk about time investment.

There are, for all intents and purposes, three types of ads. The Sponsored Product ads are more commonly referred to as keyword ads. On the Product Display side, there are two choices, interests and products.

The keyword ads and products ads take a long time to build (or do they?!…that's a teaser).

I'll be talking about how I create my lists of keywords and products and the tool I use to make it much easier. It still takes time, though it takes less now than it did when I originally wrote this chapter. More on that later.

If you haven't started binge watching Game of Thrones, it might be a good time to begin because you've got a good deal of monotonous searching to do.

Interest ads, on the other hand, take about three minutes. They are incredibly easy. The downside is that the list of available interests doesn't work for some authors. I know of an author who was disappointed to find that he was unable to target the LGBT or African American communities and another who struggled with targeting for her Christian novels. The interests are limited but they do offer one great advantage even if targeting isn't exact. They're the ads that show up on some types of Kindles.

## What are keywords and products?

My list of products is a subset of my list of keywords. This is important to consider and understand. If you spend a whole bunch of hours building a list of book titles that are similar to the book you wish to advertise, you're also creating a nice pile of keywords.

Furthermore, the author names of these book titles also make for fine keywords.

However, not all keywords are products. In the forthcoming example, I'll be building both a keyword list and a product list for my *Henry Wood Detective* series. The keywords mystery, detective, thriller, are NOT products.

It's like the rule in geometry, all squares are rectangles but not all rectangles are squares.

Knowing that the following steps take time, you'll want to save your lists in an Excel file. Once you've built up thousands of products and keywords, you'll be able to run ads much more quickly. This one time building effort will serve you well into the future.

I use a tool called KDP Rocket. Link to Dave Chesson's KDP Rocket Http://briandmeeks.com/ams-mastering-amazon-ads-links/

Before I go on, please indulge me a little digression. I love KDP Rocket now but late last year I had trouble with the software.

In November of 2016, I was doing a deep study of keywords and KDP Rocket was recommended as a helpful tool for such research. Anytime I can find a new method to speed up a process or make it more effective it's a win.

A little investigation and I found that KDP Rocket was $97.00 to purchase and they offered a 30-day money back guarantee. Since there wasn't any risk to checking it out I went ahead and bought a copy.

It didn't take long to download and get going. After only one hour of use I became frustrated because the results that were being returned were mostly blank cells. My assumption was that the scraping code was outdated and that the tool may have once worked great but it no longer did the job.

It was a good thing they had a money back guarantee.

My first interaction with Dave Chesson, the creator of KDP Rocket, was to ask for a refund. He responded almost immediately, which impressed me, and processed the refund.

Not only that, but his reply was friendly.

Now, move forward to February 27, 2017. I was talking on the phone with my author buddy and she had just had a conversation with Dave. She happened to mention that he had just done a rebuild of KDP Rocket.

This intrigued me.

During my first trial, I had liked how the tool worked and what it offered. I was disappointed to have to ask for a refund. If he had calibrated the tool to work better, then I wanted to give it another try.

There was a slight hiccup with getting my licensing key. I wrote to customer service to ask for help and again Dave was right there to get me my key. Point for Team Chesson.

The first thing I did was to listen to the instructional videos. They were really well done and got me up to speed quickly. I'd give the videos an A+ for quality.

You might be wondering where I found the videos, or more accurately, where you would look to find them should you give the product a try. Well, here is where Team Chesson gets another point. There are three giant buttons on the main page and below them, next to the "EXPORT" button is a button called "VIDEO TUTORIAL" for the training videos. They are not hidden in a drop-down box or link on some help page, they're right up front so you'll never have a hard time. I love that.

After only 20 minutes of using the video, I was thrilled

with the results. The tool did all of the things I had hoped it would do the first time I tried it. Now it's part of my routine and saves me a ton of time.

Well done, Team Chesson!

If you're interested in trying out KDP Rocket, click here. (Note: This is a link to do a 30-day Risk Free Trial. This IS an affiliate link and if you buy a copy I will make money, which I will one day use to buy something I don't need.)

So, back to the task at hand, creating a list of products and keywords to test out in my ads.

The first button on the tool is the idea search. You know what I did? As the great Yogi Berra said, "When I get to a fork in the road…I take it." When I get to a button on a page, I click it.

A pop-up box appears and you simply put in your first keyword idea.

I prefer to start with the first keyword used in my book's metadata. Do you remember when you set up your book to publish on Kindle? Yes, those seven keywords are a great place to begin. My first word is "mystery."

I typed it in and then, and I love this small detail on the

tool, hit the button that reads "GO GET EM ROCKET!" They could have used something like "submit" but that wouldn't have filled me with the child-like glee I get each time I hit the button. You see, I always say, "Go get em rocket," out loud as I hit the button. I'm weird. It's fun. One more point for Team Chesson.

It feels like KDP Rocket is my little friend who is running off to help me find new ideas.

When my little rocket friend is done, there is a list of similar words to mystery. The first three for this search are mystery books, mystery novels best sellers, and mystery Babylon Joel Richardson. In total, there were over 100 results.

The next step is simple...but I'm not going to tell you it yet, he said with a teasing come- hither look.

Before we get to that simple next step I want to discuss two important things for the people who are like me when they read a how-to book. Some of us don't have the patience to wait until we've read the entire chapter to get started.

Please read the entire chapter before going crazy with this stuff.

I anticipate that some of you may have already clicked on

the link above and bought the tool because you're incredibly eager to get to the "Crushing it" stage of your book business. If you're like me (short, middle-aged, balding, in search of a super model girlfriend with a PhD in physics and a 3 handicap) you'll dive in and run amok. That's how I do new things.

It always comes back to haunt me.

What I want for you is a clean start to the process that will serve you well into the future. To achieve such a goal, you must think about two things.

    1. How am I going to store my data?
    2. How should I name the files?

As with everything in my life, the answer to the first question is Excel.

You'll want a single Excel file with all your keyword data. You can build it yourself and I'll tell you what columns I personally used to get you started.

The second question may not seem like a big deal. Please read the next bit carefully and then use this knowledge the rest of your life.

I speak of naming conventions. It's a skill I learned while building databases. When choosing variable names do it in such a way that like variables have similar beginnings. This helps to group them in the future. It's the same way with your Excel file.

You'll be creating a lot of downloads from KDP Rocket and each one needs to be named. Do not just pick the first thing that pops into your mind.

Why?

When the folder (please create one just for keyword and product data) that contains all of your downloads gets many dozens or hundreds of files, it can be hard to find an individual file if all of the file names are different. This is important because you may need to revisit a saved download if your data gets lost or you may forget which searches you've already done. If you have a proper naming convention then it will be easy to scan the files to find the old data or to learn if that search has already been completed.

Also, if done correctly, you'll be able to sort the files in the folder by clicking on the "Name" column in the folder. When you open any folder, you'll have "Name, Date Modified, Type, and Size."

So, the naming convention I use and the "simple next step" I mentioned before I went on my little rant about the beauty of naming conventions is shown below.

After Rocket has returned your "Idea Search," you simply hit the "EXPORT" button at the bottom of the results to the left of the waving astronaut.

When you've done this KDP Rocket will ask for a file name. For all my files that are done through KDP Rocket "Idea Search" I start the file with Keyword_Name of Keyword Used in Search. For this search the name is Keyword_Mystery. If it were a long tail keyword, the file might be named Keyword_Lizards Are Adorable. (Get it...? Lizards have long tails...I crack myself up.)

For my product searches, I name the files Books_Author Name. We'll discuss those searches later.

Okay, so just to make sure we're clear you've done the following:

1. Clicked on "New Idea Search"
2. Chosen a keyword from your book's KDP setup list
3. Typed that word into the search
4. Waited for the search to complete while humming The Girl from Ipanema
5. Hit the "EXPORT" button near the astronaut
6. Gave your file a name that starts with Keyword_

It is time to talk about some general ideas for creating

your Excel keyword tracking workbook.

The easiest thing to do is take your first download from KDP Rocket and use it as the starting point.

Go ahead and open the file. I'll wait.

There are six columns. They are Keyword, Competitors, Average Earnings, Google Searches, Amazon Searches, and Competition Grade.

Raise your hand if you're considering deleting all the columns other than keywords?

Okay, to those of you who did not raise your hand, you're getting ten extra points on your mid-term exam.

For the readers who thought they would keep things simple by getting rid of all the extra wonderful and useful data, I want you to take a moment to think about what you've done.

Now, go write on the chalkboard, "I love data" 100 times.

The reason we keep all those extra columns is that one may never know how they might come in handy. The competitor's column could be helpful in analyzing the keywords for other uses beyond ads. For instance, your book may have seven keywords that have 150,000 competitors each and this may not be optimal. It isn't prudent to go into strategies for picking one's keywords to give the book the best chance of success, because this is an Amazon ads book, but the work you'll be doing going through potentially thousands of keywords, will give you all the data you need for reviewing the seven words you chose.

This is actually why KDP Rocket was built. It's a great tool for picking the initial seven keywords.

The other columns could be helpful, too. If a keyword has a really high Average Earning it might be interesting to look at how that keyword performs in your ad.

Example Data Analyst Question: Is there a correlation between the Average Earnings and how well that keyword performs in ads?

If you keep this data, you will be able to do this sort of analysis.

I hope I've convinced you to keep all the columns.

The next step is to make a few changes to the workbook. (Did you already rename it?)

1. I prefer to have one column to the left of keywords. This is just a design preference. I like to

have my own numbering (instead of just the row numbers). It allows me to see how many keywords I've got on my list. Also, I want there be a little space to the left of my data purely for aesthetics.

2. To the right of the competition grade column I added "Book Title." This will let you keep all your keywords in one place. You'll be able to do a sort by the "Book Title" column to get them all grouped together. This is only important if you write more than one series or genre. I write in five plus non-fiction.

3. The next column is called 1 of 7. I simply put "yes" next to the keywords that are in my metadata on the book setup page of KDP.

4. Change the name of the tab to Keywords. The tab will have the name of the keyword search you just did. Mine read "Mystery." To change it, all you need to do is double click in the tab and it will highlight. Then type in Keyword.

This is important because we're going to be adding other tabs to this tool later.

Did you remember to hit save after those changes?

Good. Let's move on.

Now, you've got a new Excel workbook for your keywords and the results from your first KDP Rocket search.

The next step is to go through all of the results and eliminate the ones that you feel aren't going to be good for your ads. Or that's what I thought originally. Don't do this step yet. Keep reading.

As I scrolled down the results the first one that doesn't really work for me is "mystery theater." Right click on the gray Excel row number and then choose "Delete" and the row is gone.

This is how I started when doing my search but then realized that some terms were showing up on other search results, too. As I'm always interested in being efficient with my time, I now skip the steps I just told you to do and wait until the end of my keyword research.

This lets me get rid of the keywords that don't apply and also the duplicates with just one pass. I simply do a sort by the keyword and then scroll through to make the deletions. If you have "M\mystery theater" three times, then they will be grouped together and you only need to highlight all three rows and right click/delete.

The next step is to go back to KDP Rocket and choose

another keyword. Export that file and then copy the contents into your new workbook.

Make no mistake, this process takes a lot of time. If you sit down and focus you can get a whole pile of keyword to test. I, however, do not sit down and focus. I prefer to binge watch television shows on my MacBook Air, while I do the search, export, copy into workbook, drudgery. Thank goodness, I hadn't started the Game of Thrones series yet.

When you've done a bunch, and gone through them, it will be time to move on to using KDP Rocket to build a list of competitors.

Are you ready?

There are two types of data I'm going for with the second part of the tool. To the right of the orange "NEW IDEA SEARCH" button is the "NEW COMPETITION" button.

If you click on it and type "Agatha Christie" you'll be able to find books by that author. KDP Rocket goes out and returns the top 10 examples. Obviously, she produced 80 novels over her lifetime, so this doesn't grab them all, but it quickly grabs ten of them.

I would suggest you compile the ten titles of each author

who you want to target through the tool to test with your ads.

If you see through your analysis of the results that Agatha Christie titles do really well, then it is worth the time to do a manual search for all of her books and then add them manually to your workbook.

After the search is complete you are able to export the file just as you did with the keywords.

For this file I name it Books - Agatha Christie. I have no idea why I used an underscore with the keywords and a dash with the books, but I did. I'm a rebel that way. Also, I misspelled "Agatha" by adding in a bonus "t." If you make this mistake you can simply edit the file name.

Going back to your Excel Keyword workbook you'll want to add a new tab for the competition search data. The columns are different.

I'm not going to repeat the steps for doing the second tab. The rules are the same with one exception. Instead of putting the "Book Title" column to the right of the data, I added two columns to the left of "Title" and then in column B added "Book." This column is where you'll put the title of your book.

I did this because I wanted to be able to see the book title of my book next to the one from the search.

Again, it is a mystery why I did them differently. This book isn't a hard set of rules you need to follow. It's a bunch of ideas that I've tested and work for me or others. You can put your book title column wherever it suits you. Just be sure to put it somewhere because otherwise it may not be obvious which book (or series) you intended to use the keyword and titles to promote.

This means that when you copy and paste additional searches you'll need to paste the new data into column C.

Once you've done this for your books you can then run more ads. There are a lot of different theories on how to scale. It can be a challenge. There will be a whole chapter on the subject and I'll do my best to give you actionable ideas.

But wait…there's more.

Have you been patient and read all the way up to this point without stopping to do the stuff I described?

Good. You get one point.

There is something so exciting about KDP Rocket that I wanted to save it for the end. If you've tried it in the past then everything above is pretty familiar to you. Perhaps you own KDP Rocket and haven't used it in a while.

Well, the methodology I described above, while still helpful, has been relegated to my second and third plans when building a list because there is a NEW button in KDP rocket.

It is specifically designed for AMS Ads Keyword building and it is glorious.

This new feature reduced my list building from an all-day process to under 15 minutes to go from zero to 750 for my mystery series.

Using the AMS KEYWORD SEARCH button in KDP Rocket:

1. Click on the AMS KEYWORD SEARCH button (orange) in the top left corner

2. "Enter in a general keyword, phrase, or book title, and KDP Rocket will find a large list of keywords for you to use in your campaign" (That's from the tool's pop up box. All you have to do is follow the instructions. Easy peasy.

3. Hit the "GO GET EM ROCKET!" button on the pop up.

Once this is done, you'll do like you did above, save the file and then you may want to create a single file for all of your keywords. That's what I do.

In order to amass 750 keywords in 15 minutes, I did a search for "Cozy Mystery, Detective, Detective Series, Mystery, Mystery Boxed Sets, Mystery Fiction, Mystery Series, and Private Eye." That's all. I used only eight searches.

It should be noted that there were duplicates. Naturally, I did a sort and then used the following formula in the column next to my data starting on row 2, =IF(A2=A1,1,0). This may be confusing to some, but it is a great formula to understand.

My keywords were in column A. The formula, if read in English, reads If cell A2 equals cell A1, then return a value of 1, if not, then return a zero.

If all of your data is sorted by column A then only the duplicates will get ones. You can then go delete them. Or, if you want to be an Excel ninja, just copy the column with the formula you just created and in the next column, paste, special, values. This will turn the formula into actual ones and zeros. You can then sort by that new column and delete all the rows with 1s in them because those are your duplicates.

I know that some of you may be cringing at the idea of trying the formula above. I'm sorry about that. But seriously, if you spend five minutes or an hour rereading and working through those last three paragraphs until you get it to work, this one Excel tip will save you mountains of time.

The last important thing to note is that the first time you put your new list of keywords into AMS it will return errors when there are characters it doesn't allow or if there are reserved words like "Kindle or Free" that are not allowed. The easiest way to clean your list of these types of thing is to use the "Find and Replace" function in Excel. Simply highlight the column with the keywords and then use "Find and Replace" to find "Free," "Kindle," ",", etc.

Once you've removed duplicates and all the commas and other forbidden characters, and words like "Free," and "Kindle," from your list, it will be good to go. Over half of my 15 minutes was on the cleanup.

Like I said, the Ideas Search and Competition Searches features are still really valuable. They should absolutely be used when trying to figure out your keywords for your metadata when you're uploading a new book to publish, but they are now less valuable for keyword searches because of the wonderful new AMS KEYWORD SEARCH feature.

Link to Dave Chesson's KDP Rocket
Http://briandmeeks.com/ams-mastering-amazon-ads-links/

# Chapter Twenty-Five: Designing an Experiment

## Designing an Experiment

In the beginning of the book you learned how to set up your ads. Now, you've learned how to build a massive list of keywords and products. What now?

If your guess is to just run some ads and randomly pick a bid in the hope that you'll guess right, the ad will run for 12 years, lead to 783,204 sales, and a life of leisure to which you've always wanted to become accustomed.

Then you're right.

That's all there is to it.

Enjoy your summers in the Hamptons.

I would be remiss if I didn't mention that on rare occasion this strategy may not work.

Sometimes you may need to use a little thought and strategy. Again, probably 99% of you will be super rich in three or four days so you can probably skip the next bit.

If, however, you'd like to prepare for the unlikely possibility that thing may not go according to the preferred plan above, then read on.

First of all, let's talk about expectations. How long do you think your ad will generate impressions once it really gets going?

I don't know what you guessed, but you're wrong. It will be much less time than that.

For me, an ad that runs for a week or two with lots of impressions per day (say 25,000 on a Product Display – Interest ad) is one that I would call a success. Sometimes they run longer, other times seven days and they're done.

What percentage of the ads you run do you think will generate impressions?

Buzz...wrong again. I know the little voice in your head

said, "100%...duh. Why wouldn't they all run?"

The nature of what I want to teach you will be that we are trying to build a methodology that allows us to bid correctly. This means that sometimes we will be wrong and bid so low that there aren't any impressions to be had at that price.

Did you just sigh?

Yes, I think you did.

Okay, again, I know what you're thinking. It takes forever to build a list of keywords and products. I can't spend 7 hours on ads that don't work. I have to feed my children.

First of all, aren't there automatic food systems that can drop the pellets into a bowl in their cages? I honestly don't know as I've never had the children things.

I digress.

Please don't forget that all the effort you put in or are planning on investing to build your keyword and product list is not time you need to reinvest with each new ad. Also, and this is important, keyword ads are not the only type of ad to run.

Yes, I know everyone talks about keyword ads. Yes,

everyone says Product Display – Interest and Product ads don't work. Yes, I know your mind is going to focus on keyword ads because you're pretty sure that they are the only way to go.

But they're not. Again, I'm writing this chapter to explain a methodology for building a test, and I'll be using keyword ads as the example to keep your head from exploding. (Note: Numerous tests have shown that authors whose heads have exploded find their ad-producing efforts diminish rapidly from that point forward.)

So, enough rambling on.

Let's create an experiment.

Step 1: Choose your books.

You'll notice I chose books. This is important because my goals for this test are twofold. One, find the optimal bid for different keywords, and two, make a profit.

Because making a profit on this test is secondary, I'm going to be advertising books I won't necessarily advertise once the test is done and I've learned what I need.

So, the books in this test are as follows (and in this order):

1. *Henry Wood: Time & Again* (book 2 in the series) $3.99

2. *Henry Wood: Perception* (book 3 in the series) $5.99

3. *Henry Wood: Edge of Understanding* (book 4 in the series) $5.99

4. *Henry Wood Detective Agency* (book 1 in the series) $4.99

5. *Henry Wood Detective* boxed set (books 1 - 4 in the series) $8.99

The order is important. I'm going to run five ads. Each ad will use exactly the same set of keywords. There are 188 keywords in the list, which is a number I picked at random...just because that's how I roll.

Now, I'll also be using nearly identical ad copy. Each one will be slightly different because they're different books, but the overall feel will be the same. My daily budget for each ad will be $50.00

Step 2: Run ad for Henry Wood: Time & Again.

I've chosen Sponsored Product, manual keyword. I have not included the suggested keyword for this test, and then

I copied and pasted my 188 words into the manual entry box and bid .12.

Remember, this book is priced the lowest of the group so it has the lowest bid of this test. All 188 keywords will be sitting there waiting for Amazon to give it impressions with a .12 bid.

Because this is the second book in the series, it is more likely to not get a sale. It may lead to some people going to book 1 in the series, which is fine, and will muddy any ROI data for the book 1 ad, but that's okay because profit on this test is secondary.

## Step 3: Run ad for Henry Wood: Perception

There isn't anything different in this ad other than a slight tweak to the copy and the bid is now .15.

## Step 4: Run ad for Henry Wood: Edge of Understanding

Same as above with a bid of .20.

It should be noted that the margin for Perception and Edge of Understanding is $4.15 per book. If someone does buy these books the chance for a solid ROI is still pretty good. Also, the KU page reads on them are both good because the length of the books are 84K and 102K, respectively.

## Step 5: Run ad for Henry Wood Detective Agency

Now, this is book one in the series. It only has a margin of $3.45 but with read through possibilities (something that technically would exist no matter where one starts) the margin is really quite good. It can handle a higher bid.

The bid is .25. Before this test, I had never bid over .17 in two years, and I'd only done that twice over 700 ads. In fact, all of these ads are higher bids than I typically make but they are much closer to what the general public seems to bid, so I wanted to do this test for the book and my own edification.

## Step 6: Run an ad for Henry Wood Detective boxed set.

This ad's bid is .30.

The little voice in my head says I'm crazy. Still, there are countless other authors who are bidding much higher than this and the point of testing is to find out if this type of bid is worthwhile.

## Step 7: Review the data.

This is a crucial point in this chapter. I want to talk about what I'm trying to find out.

To review, I will have data on 188 keywords at five different bid points. This is significant because each of the ads will be live simultaneously and since they are for different books they will behave independently.

A good data analyst will make assumptions ahead of time and then compare the results to those guesses. This is where the enlightenment comes in and when it starts to become fun.

Yes, data can be fun.

Okay, let's think about an individual keyword.

1. The keyword with the highest bid, the one at .30 will get the most impressions.

2. The order of impressions should be in descending order from the highest bid to the lowest.

3. The CTR should be similar across all the ads.

4. The first book in the series and the boxed set should have vastly more sales than books 2, 3, and 4.

5. The actual cost per click should also move in

descending order from the top bid to the bottom bid.

Now, those are the data analyst's thoughts. There is also a personal guess that is likely going to be wrong. I'll have a horrible ROI on the boxed set. I'll spend a fortune on the ad, and end up barely breaking even or worse, losing money, and then spend 30 minutes curled up in the fetal position weeping softy.

Let me tell you why I may be wrong about such a crazy bid. First of all, the maths (Yes, I put an "s" on it so that you'd read that bit with an English accent. Everything sounds better with an English accent.)

I know my conversion rate is around 1:10. That says to me that over the long run I'll spend $3.00 on clicks to get $6.25 in revenue. (Note: Page reads are almost the same amount if I get a KU download and they read the whole book, so for the sake of ease, I'll just work with the $6.25 number.)

The ROI = ($6.25 - $3.00)/$3.00 or 108%.

I can live with 108% ROI all day long. That being said, for years I've been getting .08 - .12 cent clicks for the same book. I'll let you do the ROI calculation on those ads. The short answer is it's a big pile of money.

Nobody should complain about 108% ROI but the point of the test is to figure out how to maximize our profits. There is an old saying that is important to learn now and to take to heart. "Make hay for feeding the guinea pigs while the sun shines."

You do NOT want to find out you've been overpaying for clicks for years when the day comes that there is a change and suddenly you're only able to manage a meager 10% ROI.

Again, one shouldn't cry over 10% either. Warren Buffet would jump for joy at a 10% profit for an entire month and he's had years that were 7% and compared to the market it was still a massive win. 10% in one day is fantastic, but right now 100 – 300% can happen too.

Let's take a moment to think about really high bids. Imagine a bid of .75 per click.

Now, when people make these bids they usually end up paying less, often much less, say .45 per click.

What is going on when a person outbids everyone else?

The belief is that they are getting their ad served first. If this is the case and the keyword is sufficiently popular to have lots of available impressions per day, then this "top bidder" will easily spend their daily budget in its entirety.

Imagine a .75 bid and an actual cost per click of .45 with a budget of $25.00. That person will get, in theory, get impressions until they've received 55 clicks. For keyword ads, that's going to be somewhere in the neighborhood of 55,000 impressions.

So, if the system works according to the above rules that Amazon is only factoring in bid, then if there are 100,000 impressions there will be 45,000 impressions left over for whomever has the next bid, presumably at .44 cents.

I don't believe that the system is this cut and dried.

A data analyst only needs to prove a single instance of the rules not working to conclude that the system is not purely bid only.

If one of my keywords (Tom Clancy) gets impressions on the ad with the .30 bid and it is truly a pure bid system, then that ad and the keyword Tom Clancy will get clicks until my budget for all 188 keywords in that ad is exhausted. If it was the only keyword that would mean that 166 clicks from roughly 150K – 200K worth of impressions would happen before the keyword Tom Clancy in the ad with the .25 bid saw a single impression.

What is the least proof I need to say that it isn't a purely bid system?

I would think if there are impressions and clicks for a single keyword across multiple ads where the most expensive ad did NOT reach its $50.00 daily budget bid.

Anyone who has already run some ads knows that spending their entire budget is rare. I don't have any expectation that I'll come close to maxing out my budget. If I do, I'll be celebrating.

What is more likely is that the budget won't get maxed out. There will be numerous keywords that have impressions and clicks across all five ads.

I suspect Amazon delivers ads based upon many criteria. This test won't shed light on the details of their criteria but it may prove it isn't a pure bid system.

The next thing I want you to think about is if there is enough data to get a feeling for the different plateaus. What I mean by this is say the .30 bid gets me clicks at .22. My next question would be "Can I bid .21 and still manage to get as many impressions delivered? Or will the .21 bid get me impressions at .18?"

If one gets enough data then it will be possible to build a more nuanced (and profitable) strategy.

# Chapter Twenty-Six: Letter to

# Authors

Dear Author,

You've reached the end of the book but not the end of the journey. AMS marketing takes a lot of effort. In fact, now that you've reached the end of the book, if you wanted to know what I'd recommend doing next, I'd say, start with Chapter 4 and reread one chapter per day until you've gotten though the book again.

There are a lot of details and few people will remember everything. Yet, you must know it all if you truly want to crush it in this business. You can't leave out the bit about optimizing your description, or gloss over the section on Random Days of Awesome. If you can't duplicate my analysis with your own ads, then you need to learn by doing.

It will take a while. One reader devoted many hours per day from late Feb until Late June and then wrote me to share her results. Her previous best sales for a month BB (Before Book) was $265. She expects to pass $7,000 for June. Don't be fooled, she's worked really hard and ran hundreds of ads.

At this point, seasoned authors would expect a page in the back matter that lists my other books.

They would also expect a call-to-action to get you on my list.

Here is the thing, I'm all about data, as you know by this point. I want to track everything, so, if you're interested in more books I've written on the subject of the book business, then follow this link:

Http://briandmeeks.com/non-fiction

Why make us follow a link?

Because affiliate links are not allowed in Kindle books. The links on the page will allow me to see if there are any sales that come from readers of Mastering Amazon Ads: An Author's Guide. This will give me more data.

As for the second point, yes, I really should be trying to get your email address. But instead I'm going to tell you about a group I have on FB called *Mastering Amazon Ads: An Author's Guide – Beta*. It's more of a lab for doing research on Ads specifically and also the book business… like "How many people who made it to the back matter of MAA then went on to buy one of my other books?"

So, this may be the worst back matter ever. Or, maybe it will be invaluable in learning information that will ultimately profit me (and the group) more. We don't know.

All I do know is that I appreciate you reading the book. There is still much to learn and discover. And if you want to be a part of that, then go look up the FB group.

Sincerely,

Brian D. Meeks

p.s. If you are interested in my fiction books, of which I have 13, then you'll just have to go find them on Amazon. I also write under Arthur Byrne. But seriously, you should be writing NOT reading my silliness.

32916869R00149

Made in the USA
Middletown, DE
09 January 2019